Ecocities Illustrated

*the easily built
visionary future of
Richard Register*

Copyright © 2016 Richard Register

All rights reserved.

ISBN-13: 978-0692747520

All drawings by Richard Register

Book design and layout by Creative Juices: www.cjuices.com

Ecocity Builders, 339 15th St., Oakland, California 94612, USA
More information from: www.ecocitybuilders.org

Dedication

This book is dedicated to Richard's friends the plants and animals.

Table of Contents, Ecocities Illustrated

Introduction	9
1. Basic Principles	12
1.1 Ecocity San Francisco	13
1.2 Bio and cultural diversity	14
1.3 Comparative layouts, sprawl, medium, dense	15
1.4 Slabs and towers, and, ecocity cross section	16
1.5 a Skycourts, towers and pedestals merging into fractals	17
1.5 b Fused towers and pedestals becoming an ecocity fractal	18
1.6 a Five blocks condensing to one block	19
1.6 b Close up, same volume and types of useable space	20
1.7 Understory, canopy and emergents	21
1.8 a Temperature and moisture layering, nature	22
1.8 b Temperature and moisture layering, city	23
1.9 Shaban (Yemen) effect: density temperature inertia	24
1.10 Keyhole plaza – people, culture and nature celebrated together	25
2. Strategies for communicating	26
2.1 Zoom through arcology in hills	27
2.2 a Sequential downtown transformation, initial condition	28
2.2 b Downtown transformation, under construction	29
2.2 c Downtown transformation, ecocity details and arrangement	30
2.3 Densifying toward centers, de-densifying farther out	31
2.4 a Transect, downtown to medium density and close up, below	32
2.4 b Transect from medium density to rural and ecovillage	33
2.4 c Pedestrian accessibility, carcity vs. ecocity in downtown	33
2.5 Height, sunshine and shadow envelopes	34
2.6 Visible nature in cities: large trees high in buildings	35
3. Full-on Ecocities	36
3.1 Whole city in its environment	37
3.2 Height limit envelope	38
3.3 Four maps for directing development	39
3.4 Keyhole plaza from two perspectives	40
3.5 a Keyhole plaza town – a model, not a drawing	41
3.5 b Elevated plaza views, bridges, skylight	42
3.5 c Interior skylight illuminated halls, "dark zones"	43
3.6 a Huaibei overall perspective	44
3.6 b Huaibei – people, bridges, elevators	45
3.6 c Active and passive solar energy	45

3.6 d Natural, agricultural and ornamental green — 46
3.6 e (1) Arts: gates, sculptures, steps, windows, balconies, walls — 46
3.6 e (2) Zooming in on the arts features image from p. 46 — 47
3.6 f Huaibei steps cross section — 47
3.6 g View from Huaibei steps — 48
3.6 h Architects' clusters, gates and views — 48
3.6 i Views celebrated through the openings of the keyhole plazas — 49
3.7 Village and town for the Future of Cities Conference — 50
3.8 Semi-dry region town at night — 51

4. Ecocity mapping and rising into the third dimension — 52
   4.1 a Ecocity map, working copy for Berkeley — 53
   4.1 b Applying the map over time — 54
   4.2 a Metropolis: NASA satellite photo of the San Francisco Bay Area — 55
   4.2 b Ecotropolis: City, major district and neighborhood centers — 56
   4.2 c Ecotropolis: nature and agriculture return — 57
   4.3 Roll back sprawl — 58
   4.4 Transferring density — 59
   4.5 Where not to build — 60
   4.6 a Suburb in foreground, distant small town changing — 61
   4.6 b Shifting to ecocity and open space, 30 years later — 61
   4.6 c Shifting to ecocity and open space, 75 years later — 62
   4.7 a DMZ town, expanded natural area (Demilitarized Zone, Korea) — 63
   4.7 b DMZ town on coastline — 64

5. Arcologies — 65
   5.1 Zoom through prairie town — 66
   5.2 Hot climate city by night – to catch the breeze — 67
   5.3 a Tableland — 68
   5.3 b Tableland with built community — 69
   5.4 Sky lobby — 70
   5.5 a Three climates Arcologies, temperate — 71
   5.5 b Hot climate, shade structures — 72
   5.5 c Cold climate, heavy on the solar greenhouses — 73
   5.6 Semi-arcology, Santa Cruz — 74
   5.7 Town as hill, Gene Zellmer inspired — 75

6. Fractals — 76
   6.1 Integral neighborhood for West Berkeley — 77
   6.2 A step on the way: a work-live, multi-family country house — 78
   6.3 Almost a fractal — 79
   6.4 Big block downtown fractal with grand hallway — 80
   6.5 Town of bridge-linked fractals — 81
   6.6 a Heart of the City Project design for downtown Berkeley — 82
   6.6 b Same site and variety of functions, extra modern — 83
   6.6 c Same site with favorite Arts and Crafts style — 84

6.6 d Same site, again, with usual city variety	85
6.6 e Circulation: bridges, ground level, rooftops, water	86
6.6 f Addison St. bridge building, Heart of the City Project	87
6.6 g Sixth Floor Street Café, Heart of the City Project	88
6.7 a & b Implantations added to a city	89
6.8 a & b Implantation with subway train leaving the center	90

7. Downtowns	91
7.1 Berkeley Civic Center Park with creek	92
7.2 Rural town center with stars at night	93
7.3 San Francisco downtown with bridges	94
7.4 San Francisco, quick sketch	95
7.5 San Francisco more developed pen drawing	96
7.6 Small downtown creek environment	97
7.7 Downtown market with shade cloth and rooftop trees	98

8. Plazas	99
8.1 Arcata, California future plaza, view to hills	100
8.2 Elevated keyhole plaza	101
8.3 Union Square, San Francisco	102

9. Transport	103
9.1 Vegetable Garden Car	104
9.2 Delivery vehicles of the future	105
9.3 Bike, bus and cart	105
9.4 Future of the automobile industry, if healthy	106
9.4 Elevated bicycle freeway	107
9.5 Street becomes pedestrian hallway with skylights	108
9.6 New bridge building helps create pedestrian street	109
9.7 Installing plastic bridge between buildings	110
9.8 Flying through town	111
9.9 Car reality again	111

10. Villages	112
10.1 Ecotopian ecovillage on a bay in northern California	113
10.2 a Village, beginnings	114
10.2 b Village grows, here portrayed as an X-ray image	115
10.3 a Bicycle City	116
10.3 b Bicycle City topo map and rough layout	117
10.3 c Bicycle City's first structures	118
10.4 a Growing futuristic ecovillage maps	119
10.4 b Growing futuristic ecovillage, two elevations	120

11. San Francisco Bay and City – from metropolis to ecotropolis	121
11.1 a Rising Tides Competition entry poster	122
11.2 b San Francisco bioregional fly through	123

12. Berkeley ... 124
    12.1 Ecocity in Berkeley-like setting ... 125
    12.2 a The Marina becomes a bay village, far ... 125
    12.2 b The Marina becomes a bay village, close ... 126
    12.3 a Eco/Peace Museum and Center at Marina, sketch ... 127
    12.3 b Eco/Peace Museum and Center at Marina, line drawing ... 128
    12.3 c Eco/Peace Museum and Center inside, sketch ... 129
    12.3 d Eco/Peace Museum and Center inside ... 130
    12.4 a Car parking only ... 131
    12.4 b Cart parking, playground, garden, cafe, more people… ... 131
    12.5 Five quick sketches at a Berkeley creek meeting ... 132

13 Oakland ... 133
    13.1 a Ecocity mapping preliminary sketch for Oakland ... 134
    13.1 b Past, present and future map of Oakland ... 135
    13.2 a Mills College ecotown center on Leona Creek ... 136
    13.2 b Ecotown Mills College, new elevated plaza ... 137
    13.2 c Mills elevated plaza from adjacent lake Aliso ... 138
    13.2 d Mills Lake Aliso Nature Center ... 139
    13.2 e Mills College with new development in ecocity style ... 140
    13.2 f Mills College expanding ... 141
    13.2 g Mills College connecting to the Bay ... 142
    13.3 Grand Lake Theater area, north end of Lake Merritt ... 143

14. New Orleans, floods and other disasters ... 144
    14.1 a Basic idea for elevating land and compact development ... 145
    14.1 b Bring back natural waters and plants, make island arts ... 146
    14.1 c Hill, shell and labyrinth: solution for hurricane cities ... 147
    14.1 d New island neighborhood on dredge and fill ... 147
    14.1 e A new quarter rises on elevated earth ... 148
    14.1 f Rainbow Girl sculpture for edge of Lake Pontchartrain ... 149
    14.2 a Build on artificial fill to avoid tsunamis, too ... 150
    14.3 a Fire safe village for Mediterranean climates ... 151
    14.4 b Firefighting close up ... 152

15. Key projects underway ... 153
    15.1 a Adjusting the map of Tianjin Eco-City ... 154
    15.1 b An elevated double layered keyhole plaza ... 155
    15.1 c Amending the large buildings only, wide streets pattern ... 156
    15.2 a Location for a possible ecotown in Bhutan ... 157
    15.2 b A thoroughly pedestrian design ... 158
    15.2 c Cross section of Anala, the lower of the two town centers ... 159
    15.2 d Anala: traditional and ecocity features ... 160
    15.2 e Zooming in on rooftop details ... 161
    15.3 a Basic form of Detroit – and thousands of other car cities ... 162

15.3 b Slowly disintegrating since the 1960s — 163
15.3 c Ecocity "fractal" or whole small town within town — 164
15.3 d Plaza and street experience — 165
15.3 e Creating close-in nature and farm — 166

16. Nature and garden — 167
    16.1 Some native species, San Francisco Bay Area — 168
    16.2 Make street narrow, add orchard and food gardens — 169
    16.3 Urban street nut harvester — 170
    16.4 Orchard over freeway — 171
    16.5 Book cover for Ecocity Berkeley — 172
    16.6 Birdhouse for large urban park — 173
    16.7 Colin Davis at restored creek, Berkeley/Albany border — 174
    16.8 Space city down to earth — 175

17. Sculptural city — 176
    17.1 Nature on and all around — 177
    17.2 Rainbow prism aqueduct water sculpture — 178
    17.3 Creek environment for bioregional sculpture — 179
    17.4 Bioregional sculpture near creek — 180

Conclusion — 181
Acknowledgments — 182
About the Author — 183

Introduction

Part 1

Seeing something in the mind and working it out. That's what the artist has to do: transform the dream, vision, "content" of the idea or concept, feeling or insight, ecstasy or horror, beauty or disgust, honesty or enlightening illusion… The list goes on, but it's something from the imagination into something in the hand, before the eye, in the ear, mind or heart of the self and other. That means translating from the mind to the body, mental to physical of my own self and to someone else. Call it the community of insightful communication, the more religious might even say reverent communion. Why not try for collective ecstasy?

So I'm an illustrator of something important to me and I think everyone: how to live deep into a healthy future, something very physical in a structure built for more than just ME, but for everyone, and ultimately all life on this beautiful planet.

There's the Beauty of art, the Justice of law, the Good of the compassionate and moral, the Healthy into the future, the health, that is, of the home we build and the home we got as our birth gift called our natural environment. The Beautiful, the Just, the Good and the Healthy are ideals, moving objectives imperfectly approached, but the best of our attempts as humans. Let me know if you can think of any better.

The ideal of the ecocity – the ecologically healthy city, the city that can exist harmoniously with ecological and bioregional systems here in my part of California or anywhere in the world, the city that actually furthers healthy evolution – that's my goal. The ideal isn't a place like an imagined no place called Utopia but a lighthouse to guide our way, past the reefs and through the waters teaming with edible, watchable, enjoyable life. You don't even want to arrive at the lighthouse – too dangerous. Those who try to get too close to the lighthouse usually crash on the rocks. Very sad! But to be guiding – while avoiding the catastrophic crash – something like the lighthouse – that's what I hope and presume after all these years of efforts to be doing, at least in some degree, through these drawings and associated writings, talks, travel, photography, conference organizing – whatever seems to help.

Fanciful or realistic? All that I've drawn is easily built physically with technologies well known today and have been for a long time already – though deciding to build it is another and apparently very difficult thing. The images might look different from a lot we see today, but they do not defy gravity or depend on imagined fundamentally different materials than we have now, neither do they depend on vast personal wealth for a place in the vision nor require advanced degrees. They just have to provide most of what we need in the world we build, and *must* build, for *all* of us in full and gracious respect of universe, solar system, lithosphere, hydrosphere, atmosphere, climate system, soils, plants, animals, people. Yes, build telescopes and space ships too. But get the foundations in the dirt right. That's the most important.

Part 2

I had the good fortune to cross paths with architect/philosopher Paolo Soleri in 1965, when I was 21 years old. He said the sprawling automobile city with its paving, vast single use zones and gluttonous appetite for land and cheap energy was an enormous structure with profoundly negative implications. He said something overlooked that sounded to me like a paradox but true: despite the apparently small size of all those scattered separate individual houses in the middle of lawns and all those cars buzzing about, the suburban type of city constitutes a gigantic infrastructure. What looks large in downtown skylines are collectively much smaller for the number of people served than the infrastructure of the automobile suburb with its vast expanse of concrete, asphalt, wires, pipes, redundant – *not* shared – walls, ceilings and floors and all its vehicles demanding floods of fuel producing profound problems from local pollution to climate change, all the while displacing farmland and natural landscapes and species. He warned us of the enormous potential damage the sprawling cities of cars promised.

Soleri portrayed a very different approach, a means for further healthy evolution down the path of the city scaled to the human body, not the car body. Liberate *that*, liberate the human body through ecocity design for easy access by foot, bicycle, elevator, streetcar, personal and social transportation. The form of the ecocity is more three-dimensional like everyday complex living organisms such as our own human bodies, not flat like a sheet of paper, two-dimensional. The difference between plane geometry and geometry in three dimensions has profound implications for material and energy conservation and efficiency of a high and healthy order. Therein find some important keys to a healthy future, and even further healthy evolution of humanity and nature here on this our home planet.

I thought Soleri's thinking made enormous good sense, living in smog-strangled Los Angeles at the time I met him, praying for the western sea breeze like surfers in the same town praying for waves. Those running the city in those days recognized the smog as a Bad and clean air as a Good so they fixed the car. They put a smog device on it. They did in fact impressively improve the air quality in the LA basin and guess what? Forty-five years later, because everyone thought fixing the car instead of the city was a good idea, Los Angeles modeled the city of desire and consumerist prosperity for the rest of the rapidly growing world of cities… and brought us to the doorstep of catastrophe for all the future: climate change, rising seas, massive displacement of natural and agricultural land by asphalt and lawns, paving displacing habitat and accelerating extinctions of hundreds of species.

Unfortunately, now the ecocity isn't only the ideal of the best we can build. Even more basically the ecocity has become the city of sheer survival. We discover we need a rescue and here comes the ecocity. Either we fix the city in time or pity our children the world they will inherit. If the Earth is a living thing, pity its atmosphere its fever, its geology its pock marks of tar sand mines, its oceans their formerly normal circulation and their growing acidification, and our whole degenerating biosphere. The time is short: climate change, species extinctions, extirpation and dissipation of physical resources are moving quickly. Ecocities are not the whole answer, but without them a major opportunity for a happy future will be lost forever.

And beyond all that, cities are the containers of the fastest moving and most consequential of creative cultural environments, environments we create ourselves, that can help us evolve into our better selves.

Organization of this book

Here in this book you will see clusters of drawings organized into chapters according to various themes such as whole cities, downtowns, neighborhoods, transportation, mapping ideas, plazas, approaches to visualization such as using zooms, pans and time lapse sequenced drawings and so on. Throughout, my drawings have been not only influenced by what I hope is advanced thinking about city design informed by ecology, but also informed by the countless ecocity features I've seen in my considerable international wanderings promoting the concept. In all of this I will be treating cities as living organisms, the "anatomy analogy," with "body parts" something like organs organized three-dimensionally, not scattered flat in two-dimensions like the city built by, of and for cars. Cities have their districts with functions linked by networks. We have our organs and functions and pathways linked by veins and nerves… Long may we all thrive, us living organisms and the living city we inhabit and build. But to do that we need to explore and better understand what such cities might be like. This is my best guess.

Before I met Paolo I thought I was an artist destined to make wonderful sculpture. After thinking through the importance of reshaping cities for long range thriving of our human cultures and restoring nature to the health it deserves, I decided that designing cities, organized three-dimensionally in form something like sculptures to live in, would be the more healthy thing for me to try to do for a better future – mine and everyone else's. What you see here then is the product of that conversion to a different career than I had earlier imagined. I think it has been a helpful change for me and will help others too.

Ultimately, I believe, we all have to make changes in this direction, not necessarily by way of everyone being involved in city design, but at least understanding it and helping ecocities along while enjoying the transition to the max!

1.

Basic Principles

Everywhere on Earth climate, weather, geology, sun angles, temperature range and fluctuations, wind direction and force, precipitation, geography, ecology and human culture and tradition are different. Yet if there are core basic principles for organizing the city around people instead of machines (dominated by automobiles) we can expect the details to take form in certain patterns. We explore some of them in this cluster of drawings.

1.1 Ecocity San Francisco

I start with a drawing that has become something of an icon for my work, an imaginary San Francisco of the future – extra green, with far less commuting, unified on several levels with bridges – pedestrian permeability and no cars in town, though a few parking lots for rental cars to the country. It's a pedestrian, bicycle, transit infrastructure powered by renewable energy, largely from solar nearby.

1.2 Bio and cultural diversity

There is no reason people can't live in their own cultural diversity, drawing below, while maintaining natural biodiversity, drawing above *and* below. We will take up some space belonging formerly to the other organisms, but with a proper sense of limits and good design none should ever go extinct on our account.

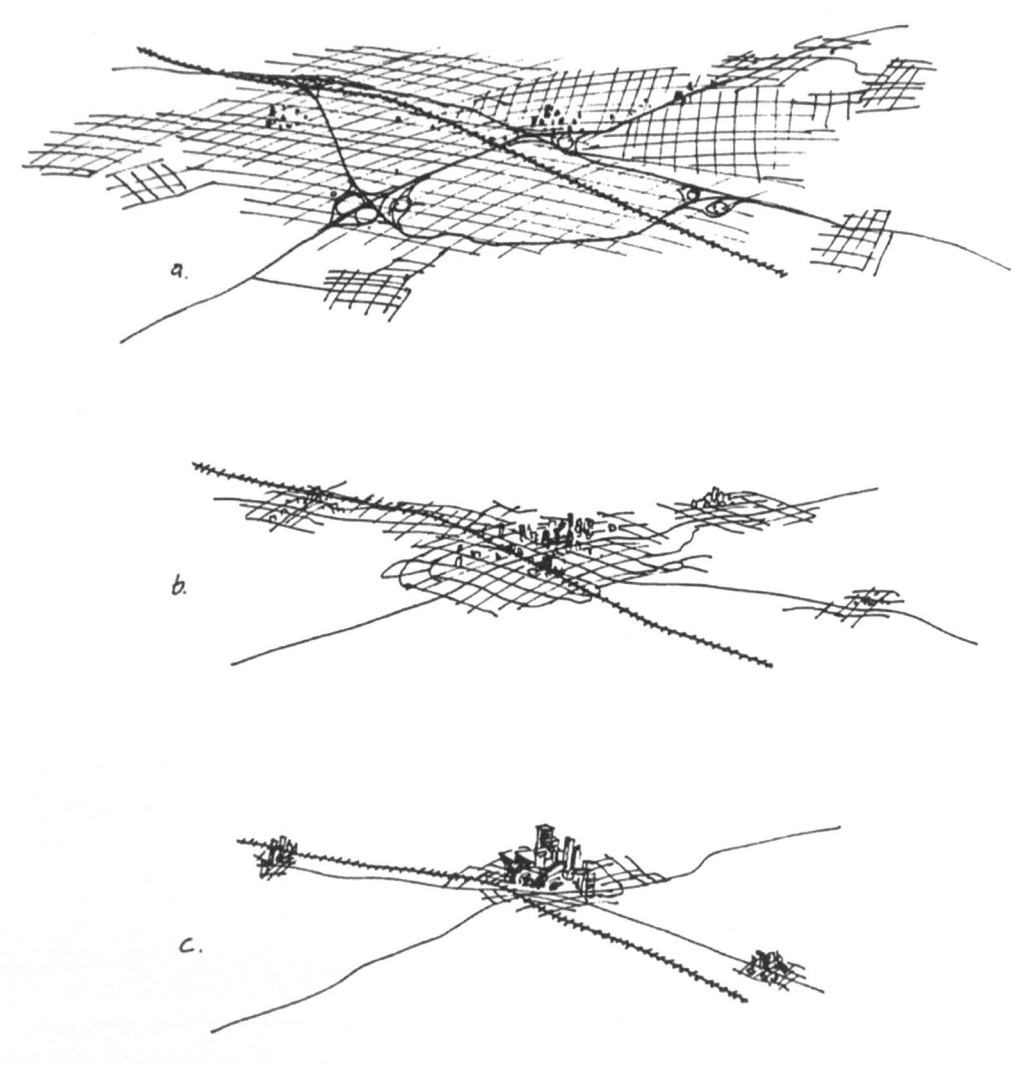

1.3 Comparative whole city layouts: sprawl, medium density, very dense

You can't get much more basic in showing the variety of layout possibilities as two dimensional – that is, basically flat, a. above – and basically three-dimensional – that is, basically form in interconnected volume. At a glance one can see the more three-dimensional form saves more energy, asphalt, land for agriculture and nature and so on. Far fewer deaths on the transport system too. Very tall buildings like the "super talls" being constructed around the world for enticing international investment and local pride and wealth concentration are essentially one dimensional – vertical – add ons to whatever form is already there.

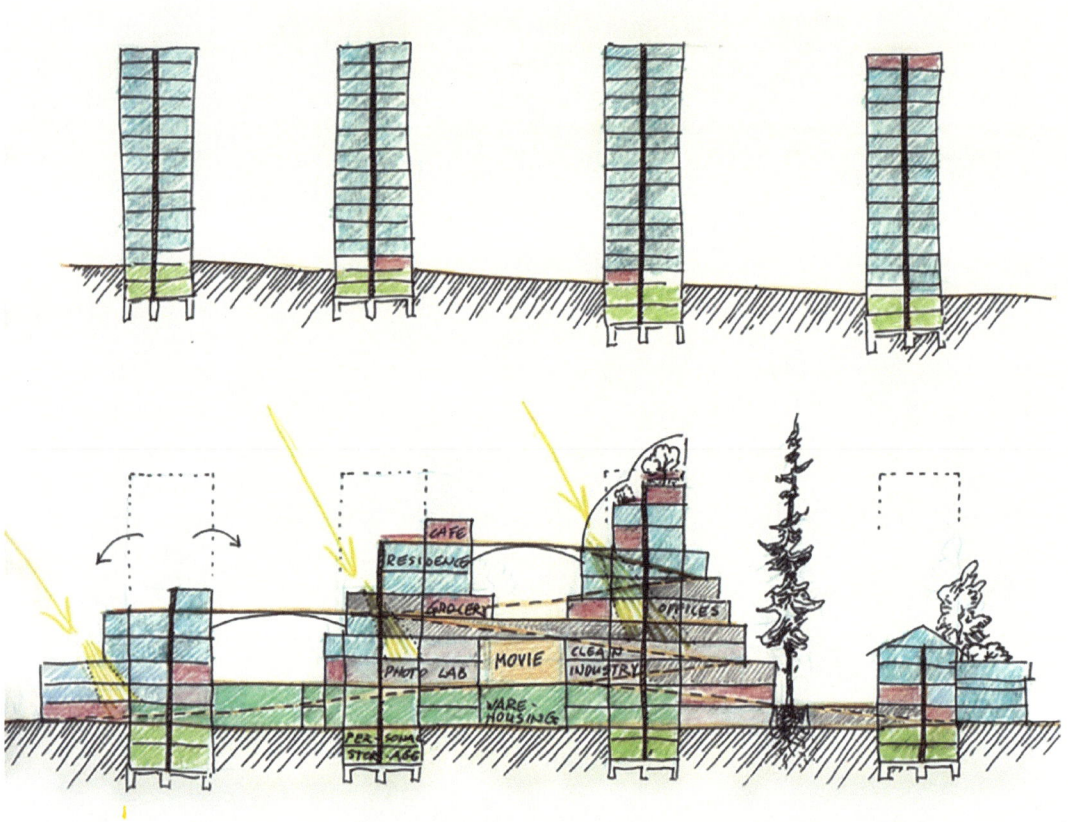

1.4 Slab and towers, and, ecocity cross section

The international style slabs and towers – simplistic "sculptures in a park" as they were characterized for some time after World War II – express the division of the city into scattered generally single uses: housing here, downtown business district there, cultural center somewhere else and industry yon, top drawing. The ecocity arrangement, lower drawing, gathers the diverse functions into close proximity. One way of looking at it is not that the shortest route between two points is a straight line but designing the points close together. The notion can be reduced almost to a slogan: "access by proximity."

Imagine supplies come into the ecocity by efficient rail mainly and warehousing is in the lower parts of the city instead of dozens of miles outside requiring collectively millions of miles of truck driving every year. Instead the town is raised a few stories and delivery is by forklift and elevator over feet and yards rather than by trucks covering vast distances.

1.5 a Skycourts, towers and pedestals merging into ecocity fractals

An ecocity "fractal" is a smaller fraction of a city serving all of the city's essential functions, with essential parts all present and well organized. Smaller than a whole city and more easily built, the "fractal" or "integral project" becomes like an ecologically informed, fully functioning village in the city and a model for thinking about whole cities as ecocities. Residential spaces, shops, offices, clean manufacturing, recreation facilities, food availability in several forms, schools, and elements of nature in that location including proper orientation toward sunshine, precipitation and views all present and properly organized.

Basic design features are illustrated here. Towers with pedestals, top left, is the design of choice for downtown buildings in Vancouver, Canada. Architect Ken Yeang of Malaysia brings air freshening vegetation into recesses in larger buildings called "skycourts," upper right, along with cooling shadows – a solution for hotter climates. In the lower left and lower right, the pedestals and towers fuse in designs with streets becoming ample interior pedestrian hallways.

1.5 b Fused towers and pedestals becoming an ecocity fractal

Zooming in to the lower right image from page 17, we can see the "mixed uses," as planners like to say, of a three-dimensional community within the larger community, shown here as linked by bridges at the third or fourth floor level of the city. That means apartments and offices, shops and all sorts of services are provided in a unified design. Studied closely we see rooftop restaurants and gardens, elevated greenhouses, streets turned into pedestrian hallways through which to move about, all in respect to the sun's position in the sky, to the left of the picture.

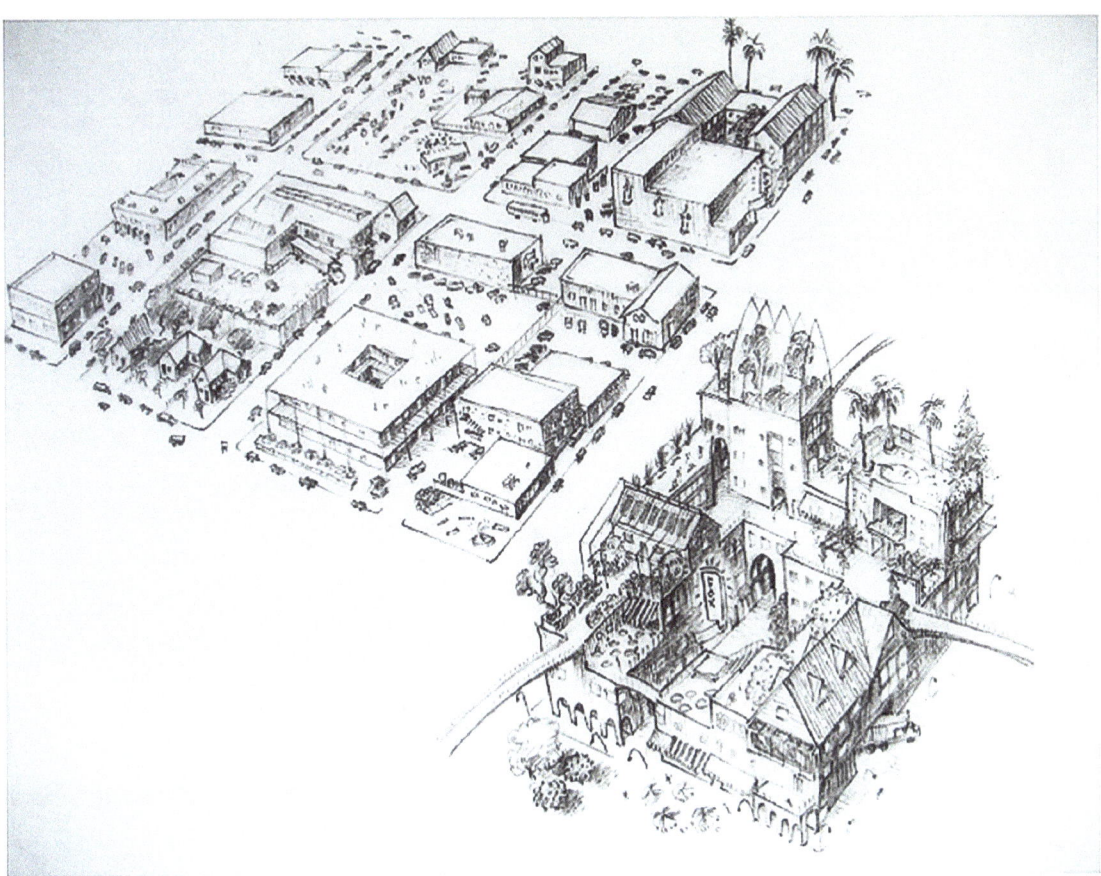

1.6 a Five blocks condensing to one block

The five block area – four plus two half blocks – in the upper left remind me of the chaos of generally low density development near Central Avenue in the city where I went to grade school, Albuquerque, New Mexico.

Imagine condensing that into one block but having the same volume of space for the functions provided in the five blocks, but minus most of the paving, trucks, redundant outside surfaces of walls and roofs. On the positive side we are adding rooftop uses and a very quiet interior surrounded by human activity instead of constantly dealing with hurtling, often noisy and smelly, sometimes fatal mechanized traffic.

1.6 b Close up, same volume and types of useable space

Zooming in for a closer look informs about the many features that are impossible in the five block area for the simple step of doing a three-dimensional design informed by ecological relationship with the surrounding resources, biosphere and community. Here we see the basically three dimensional form of the "organic" model which I think of as the "anatomy analogy."

In both the five blocks and one block version we have not only housing and shops, but also offices, restaurants, cafes, quiet interior small courtyard, rooftop gardens and small swimming pool, plus storage of things other than cars underground. The immense savings implied leave enough to splurge on the more graceful things of living together in a town or city.

1.7 Understory, canopy and emergents

For some reason, this is just one of my favorite drawings. I think it's because of the lively colors relating to one another. Also because I can see myself moving through the shady lower streets of the town and enjoying the beams of sunlight that fall there, the curiosities of the shops and people on ground level.

In the natural environment of the moist forest on the left, there is what is generally called the understory, canopy and the emergent trees that rise into the sun and breezes. This rich variety can model the way we build. As the canopy is where the action is in the forest with mammals, lizards, frogs, snakes, insects and birds clinging, crawling, zipping, hopping, flitting and soaring about, so in this drawing there are people scurrying and ambling around up on the high third and fourth floor levels on the right, with towers rising like emergents designed for pleasure as well as utility. The principle here is that in three-dimensional space various different features and functions are arranged in ways that relate to the realities of air movement, moisture level, light and heat and relationships of architectural features to one another and to connectors from streets and bridges to stairs and elevators.

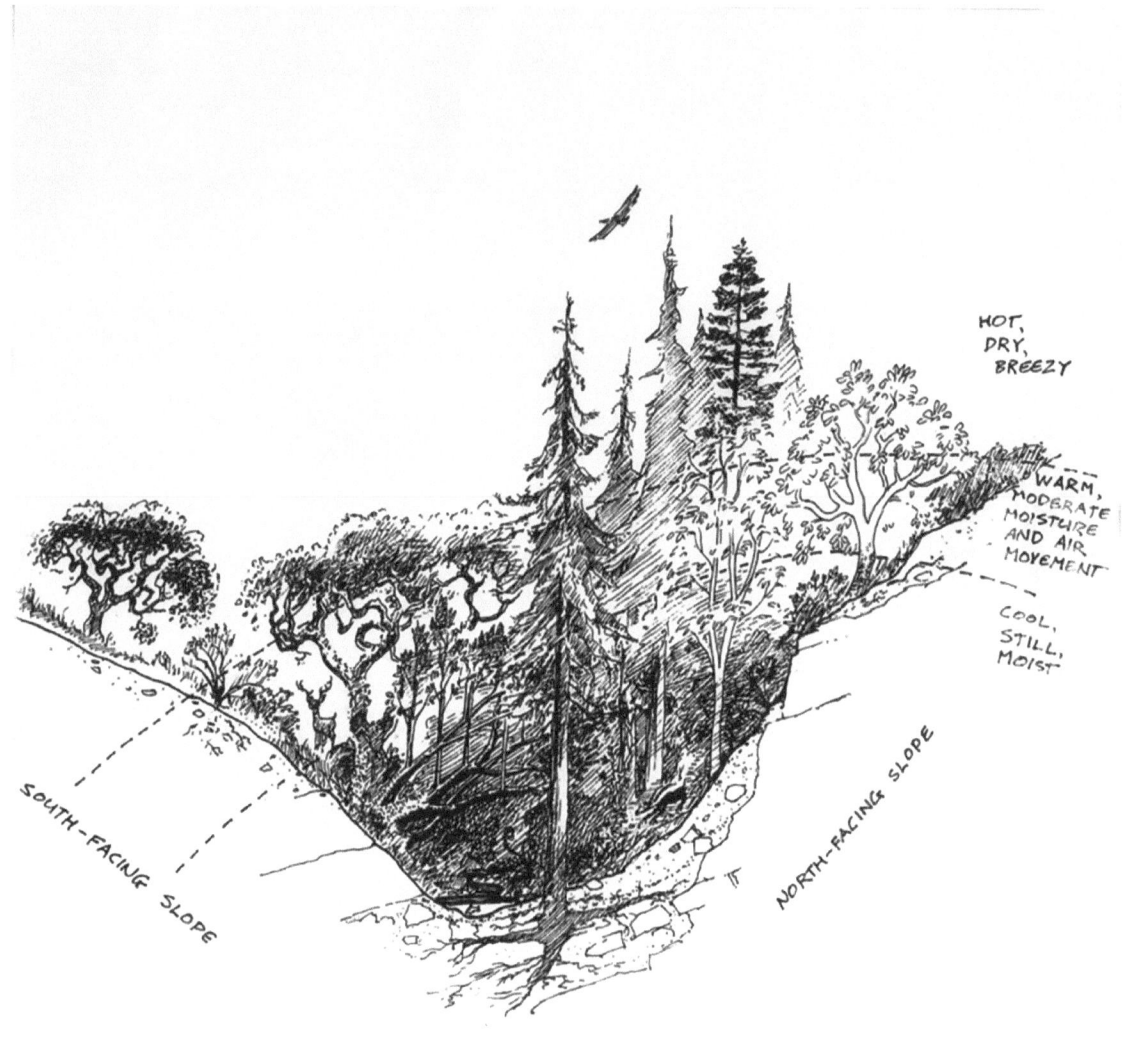

1.8 a Temperature, moisture and air movement layering – nature

In the typical kind of forest I live near in Northern California we have shady north facing slopes on the south side of valleys. There a great variety of plants grow best and the slopes stay relatively shady and moist. The sun located off-drawing to the right, oaks on the left, redwoods in the wet valley by the steeply angling bay laurel with madrone on the upper right, deer on the forest edge, skunk in the brush, hawk overhead.

1.8 b Temperature, moisture and air movement layering – city

The same hawk is flying over – of course those are schematic bridges – and we have the same layering of hotter, sunnier, breezier places above and cooler, shadier, more still places lower down. This very small plaza, just wide enough to qualify as one, opens directly from six and seven story buildings to the natural environment just beyond the sculptural fish ladder and glass aqueduct coming in to the plaza on the second story level casting rippling spectral colors into the open space floor.

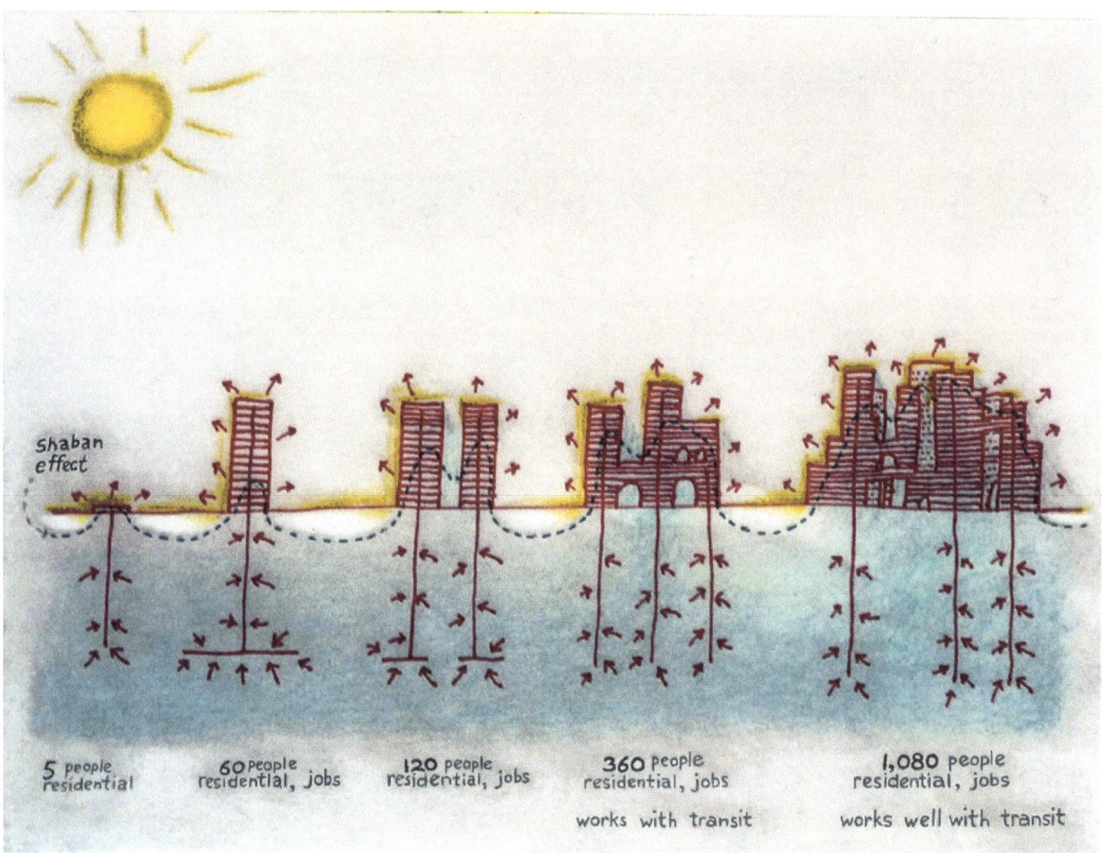

1.9 Shaban (Yemen) effect: density temperature inertia

This drawing I drew for inventor industrialist David Hall when on a trip with him to China to illustrate the use of his drilling equipment to connect compact buildings with the stable temperature of the earth below the town. His father invented industrial diamonds and David is a prolific inventor himself. The Yemen town of Shaban is made of a compact cluster of buildings generally seven to nine stories high and made of sun dried brick. It has what is called thermal inertia – that is, it tends to stay the same temperature through time due to its high total mass and the property of dried mud to change temperature only slowly.

We can see in the drawing that we can connect with the cooling effect of the earth itself which ten to twenty feet below the surface is a stable temperature day and night, and, a little deeper, stable all year around. With a large enough mass, as at Shaban where the streets are very narrow and shady, the structures cover enough of the land to bring up the coolness of the earth up into the town as if it were a small mountain. But in addition, pipes and circulating water can augment the effect. With the one story building at the left we can see it provides no shade for neighbors and loses its cooling advantage quickly.

1.10 Keyhole plaza – people, culture and nature celebrated together

    I'm not sure if this is really a principle or a design feature. Maybe both. The idea is simply to celebrate the people, the cultural product and a cherished local view all in one design. Here I imagine a coastline something like the Santa Monica, California and Pacific Ocean edge where I used to live looking up toward the mountains behind Malibu and the blue open Pacific Ocean. It is a great angle for sunsets, too.

    If we imagine looking at the old style keyhole with an opening in the middle and a wedge-shaped slot spreading out from the open space, we have the model of the keyhole plaza opening out to nature or agriculture. Place your best buildings to frame the view, not block it. The idea is to open society to the natural world, honor and celebrate it. Alternative name: view plaza.

2.

Strategies for communicating

Since the early 1970s I've been drawing my ideas for ecological cities. I've seen myself as an explorer, illustrator, sometimes inventor and educator rather than a "studio/gallery artist." I don't know if my art would be called "fine" but I believe it has important content, a message, something I'm illustrating. Maybe you could even call me a propagandist, promoter or evangelist, going to many conferences, festivals and even demonstrations, protests and – toughest of all – City Halls to put these ideas forward. The intent: getting something built.

Different people visualize and understand in different ways so I try a wide variety of approaches. You will see zoom-ins and zoom-throughs, time lapse imagery, block to block comparisons and the use of juxtaposition to stimulate some thinking, like placing extra large trees high in buildings. There are a few Photoshop projects here too. Later you'll see a NASA photograph I altered to find city and neighborhood centers in the San Francisco Bay Area. These centers could become ecocities and ecovillages in their own right, defining a new concept replacing the metropolis that I call the "ecotropolis" in its healthy "bioregion," that later term most prominently promulgated by fellow San Francisco Bay Area resident (now departed) Peter Berg. I will later show X-ray views of a village so you can see the fronts of buildings along a street through the back sides of building that would, if not treated in X-ray fashion, be in the way of what I'd like you to see. I'll save that one for later when I cover ecovillages. Novelty, spectacle and color help, so I try those off and on too. This chapter of drawings is just an introduction to various attempts to communicate the basic principles and lots of details. As a strategy throughout, I hope it works.

2.1 Zoom through arcology in hills

This sketchy drawing goes back to about 1975 thinking of what it would be like to fly like a bird approaching a Soleri-like compact city like another hill in hilly landscape. His term for such a city combines architecture and ecology: arcology.

2.2 a   Sequential downtown transformation – initial condition

We can imagine a downtown with heavy traffic, big buildings, parking lots and parking structures, smog in the air, noisy, waterways buried in pipes.

2.2 b Downtown transformation – under construction

We can also imagine transforming that to a city respecting sun angles, bringing back its waterways and heading toward being a place designed for people more so than for cars.

2.2 c Downtown transformation, ecocity details and arrangement

Here people move back into town, housing near offices, shops, food availability, practically every service needed, creating public plazas instead of parking lots. Views appear as the air pollution disappears, plants grow up, orchards in the street, waterways restored, birds of a wild variety reappear…

2.3 Densifying toward centers (light line) & de-densifying farther out

    Here we have two different ways of showing change and both moving toward a fine grain more dense version of a lively center much more pedestrian oriented than car oriented in overall design. In the top image, the light lined buildings and trees are steadily replacing the older more scattered structures shown in solid black. In the bottom two landscape cross sections, again we see the same transition but represented with the old above the new.

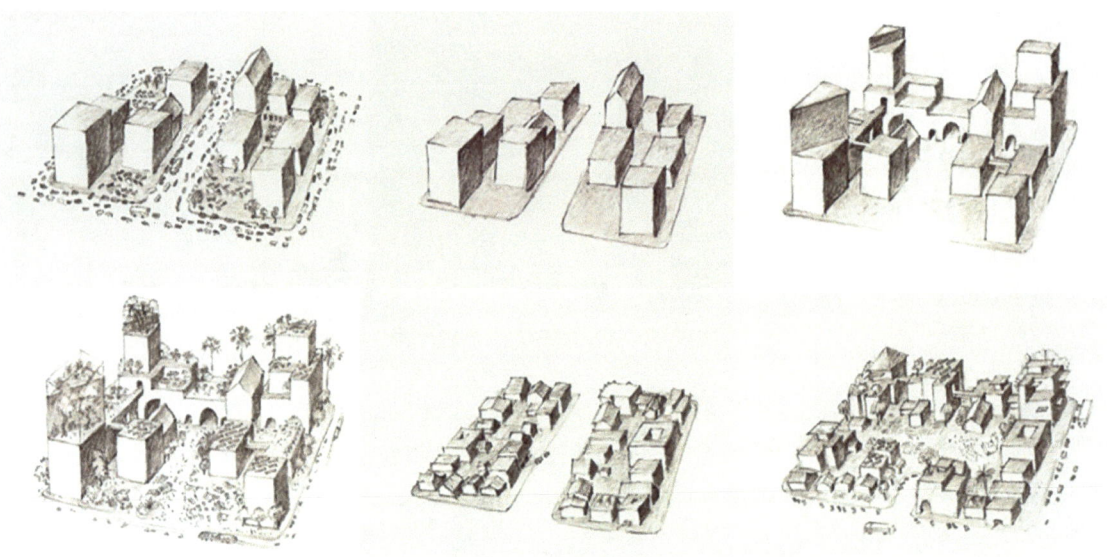

2.4 a Transect, downtown to medium density and close up, below

Left above, car city over the pedestrian city represents a downtown of fairly large buildings, remodeled and adding about 50% more capacity. The upper two images, center and right, show the basic contrasting massing with the "ecocity" design, far right, linked and unified for the pedestrian on upper level and ground level. Below you get a sense of the liveliness of the ecocity design.

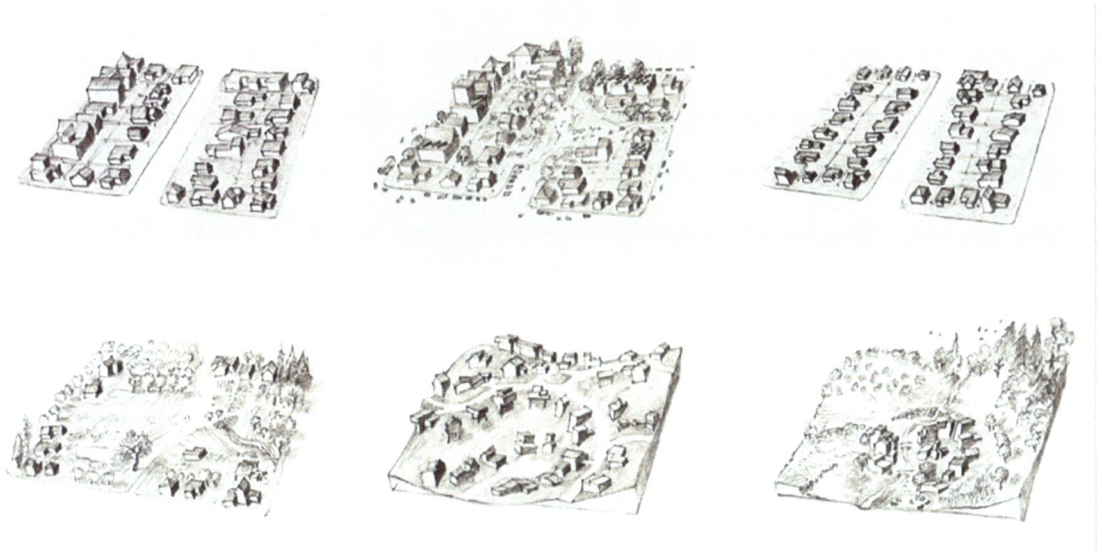

2.4 b Transect from medium density to rural and ecovillage

Here, moving out from the center, which is why we are calling these pictures a transect, slicing through the map outward, we see lower density areas going through a similar transition. Lowest density in a hilly area could be consolidated into an ecovillage while half the people move back to the city. Now it becomes real country.

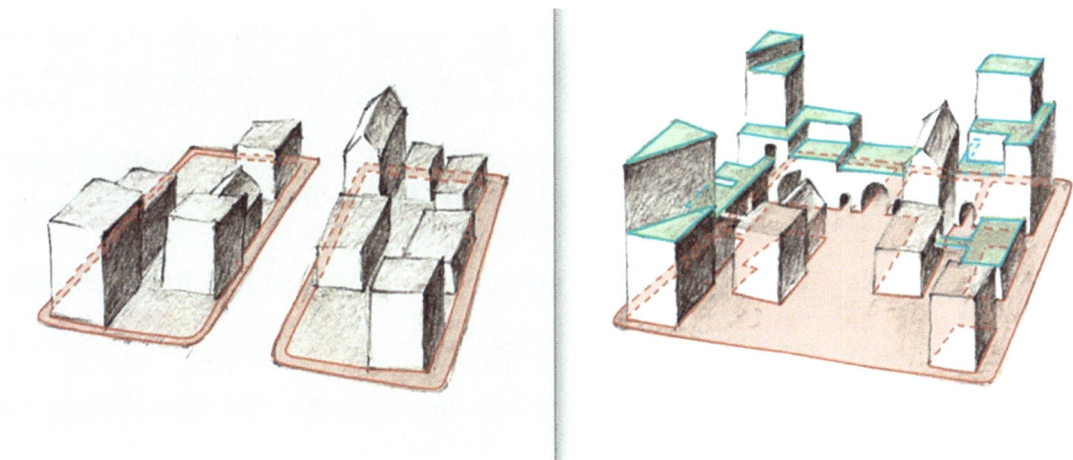

2.4 c Pedestrian accessibility – carcity vs. ecocity

Note the radically improved pedestrian access in the ecocity design on the right, two levels available for pedestrian accessibility in the whole formerly two-block area.

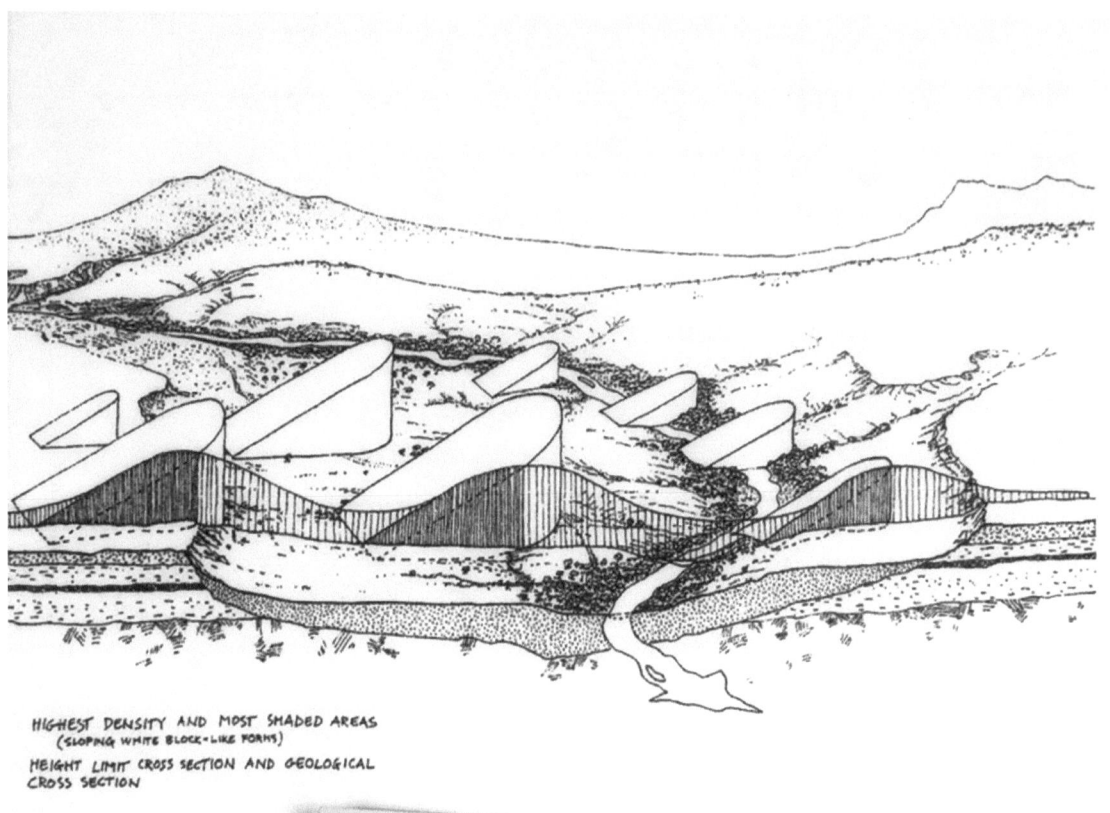

HIGHEST DENSITY AND MOST SHADED AREAS
(SLOPING WHITE BLOCK-LIKE FORMS)
HEIGHT LIMIT CROSS SECTION AND GEOLOGICAL
CROSS SECTION

2.5 Height, sunshine and shadow envelopes

This one is a little more difficult to picture. The wedges that look something like angled platforms to launch trick motorcyclists up into the air toward the right are imagined to be volumes, not solid, but closely packed buildings, very high density, in this case, on the order of twenty-five story buildings for the larger imaginary "wedges." The vertically striped wavy form is imagined height limits juxtaposed with high points coincidental to the both wedges and waves. In the areas defined by the wedges we have narrow, quiet, pedestrian streets, light bounced down with "light tubes" and reflectors and otherwise mostly artificial. This is like down at the base of the rainforest, page 21. In the areas outside the imaginary wedges the buildings can go up to the wavy line height limits but have to be spaced much farther apart for sun and breeze access to the streets and plazas.

Such artificial, built "hills" that we thus define, provide views for people on the outside surface. "Inside" we are lost among the buildings as in any dense city center today. But in this case the views are accessible to people on terraces, elevated restaurants, gardens and promenades as well as through windows. *And* the great out of doors is a short five or ten block walk, no suburbs isolating the people from getting out to the country easily and quickly. It is the best of both worlds, urban and rural, which is what the suburbs were originally supposed to deliver but failed at, making everything neither urban nor rural.

2.6 Visible nature in cities: large trees high in buildings

One device to shock people into new perspectives is placing something of nature in the highest profile – literally highest – such as on the top of tall buildings. This is what artists sometimes call a "statement," the content of which in this case is, "we honor nature here." Expensive? Yes but in the ecocity of the future we are saving countless dollars by not building the extremely expensive automobile infrastructure we had gradually gotten use to. Example: in Vancouver, Canada the tallest building at my time of writing is the Shangri-la building at 62 stories with three story tall trees on the roof protected by transparent wind screens.

3.

Full-on Ecocities

This chapter is about whole cities viewed at once, operating as compact living organisms, essentially three-dimensional in form. You will see a three-dimensional model here too, touched up electronically. I visualize variations on the theme of reshaping the city for "access by proximity," that is, designing a variety of features and functions close together. It's the city for people – the pedestrian – not the car. There has been considerable ecocity interest in the coal mining city of two million in China called Huaibei. I've suggested a small compact city for the edge of a lake on the present suburban fringe of Huaibei, the series of pictures you see in a Chinese style. In general, the style could be anything from the most traditional through contemporary into the unknown new. What is ecologically important is the creative, compassionate human environment and the maximum land left for biodiversity of nature and agriculture best use of renewable energy, and minimum use of energy in general, soils, minerals and other "resources" for all-round healthy, happy prosperity.

3.1 Whole ecocity in its environment

Here we have a city of three "hills" building out the wedges of high density toward the left of the hills' centers, which means the sun is toward the right. This image represents the "build out" of the "wedges" and hills like height limits of the cross section, illustration 2.5. Here we can see on the sunny side (right side) of the hills that the buildings are spaced to let the sun in around the towers to the streets below. A "keyhole" or "view plaza" facing us opens up to a farmland view on the left and on the right a similar plaza looks out toward the country and upstream to the local river. The height limits, maybe even requirements, of the illustration 2.5, page 34, determine the basic shape and location of the "hills." The major avenue between the "hill" on the left and the two on the right is oriented toward the mountain that dominates the horizon in the distance. From ground level at that location you could barely see the ocean at all so the view chosen to celebrate in this design is toward the mountain. Elevated bicycle and foot bridges link the three centers at about 12 stories up flying over the often labyrinthine pedestrian streets below taking bicyclists about five minutes between centers and people on foot about fifteen minutes one "hill" to another.

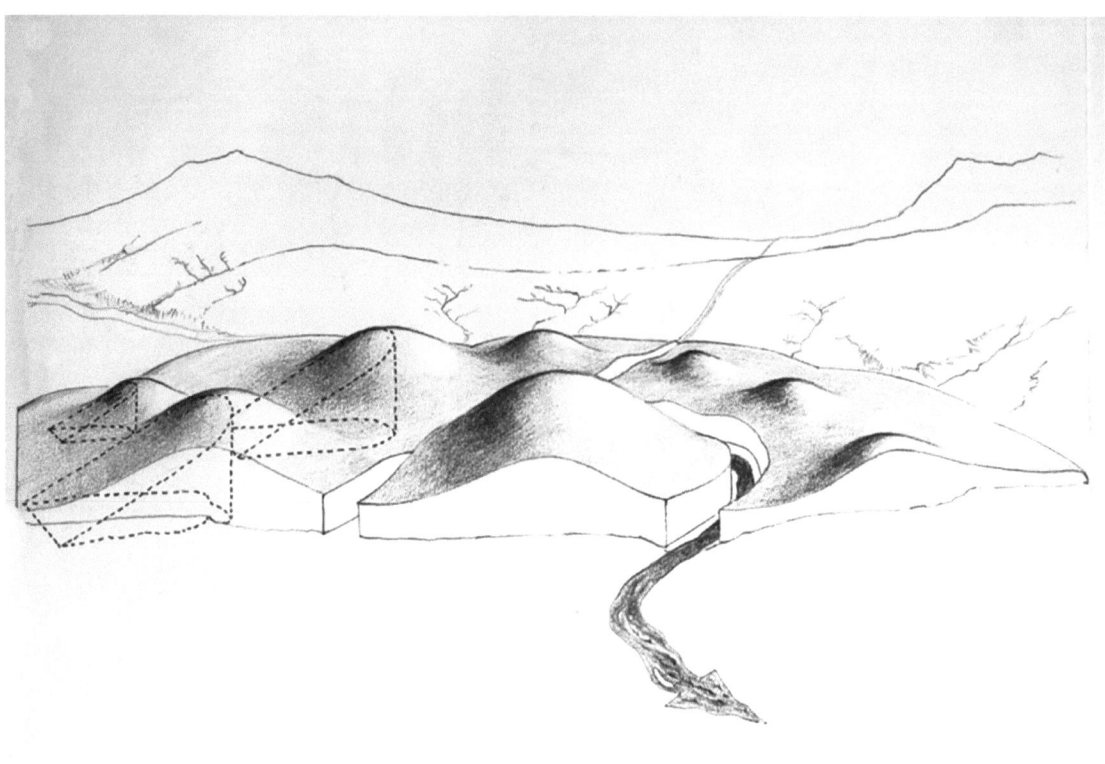

3.2 Height limit envelope

    To reiterate the height limits scheme, but this one for a more complex set of "hills." The city has a finite edge with the natural and agricultural landscape, seen at the extreme right edge of the drawing.

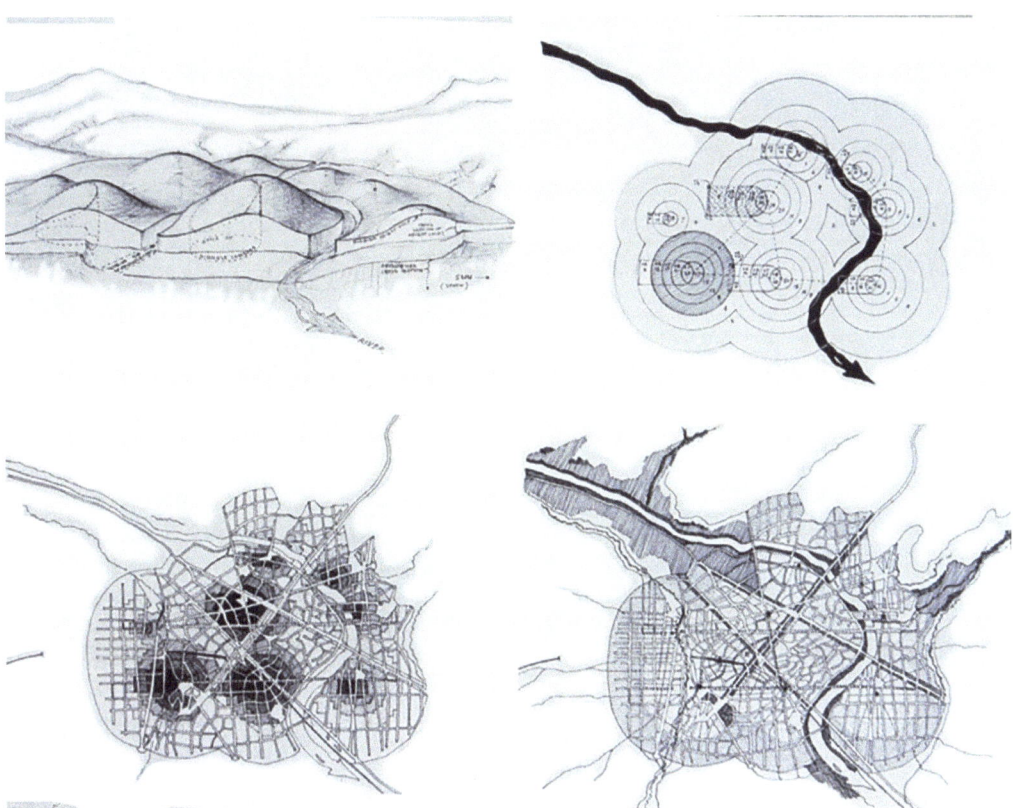

3.3 Four maps for directing development.

Top left represents the general form.

Top right lays out the basic heights and densities, heights by the target-like concentric circles, taller toward the center naturally. The bullet-like shapes are areas of highest density, defining street conditions something like interiors, but urban interiors not building interiors. The outside one or two rings could be residential only with occasional neighborhood centers with café and market and the highest density areas mainly offices and clean industry.

Bottom left shows the total population/activity averaged day and night.

Bottom right emphasizes the public parks along the river, farmland on higher banks and parks with keyhole plaza views.

This city is assumed to be in a grass and scrub oak area. The river is navigable for small ships and connects to other cities up or down stream.

3.4 Keyhole plaza from two perspectives

Another version of keyhole plaza, above, with stage and statue on left, top half of the drawing. Here I'm imagining paving with strong patterns like the Portuguese established in their colonies from Rio to Macao.

3.5 a Keyhole plaza town – a model, not a drawing

I introduced the keyhole plaza under basic principles because of its power to bring people, culture and nature together in a celebratory whole. Here, we have a whole other way of thinking of holding a city together: instead of streets and plazas, rails and bicycle routes and footpaths, for the intensively pedestrian city we have the whole infrastructure organized around a number of keyhole plazas held together by bridges, hallways, alleys, elevators and plazas people can crisscross in any direction. For heavier items, these can be backed up by small but powerful electric carts, forklifts and freight elevators replacing trucks, freeways and fuming, noisy streets.

3.5 b Elevated plaza views, bridges, skylight

Views emphasized by colors for several, but not all, of the out-facing plazas. Bridges are in orange. A large square skylight is in the center of the model. We are looking north so that the sun (in the northern hemisphere anyway) has access to the skylight most of the day, especially in the winter.

3.5 c Interior skylit halls, "dark zones"

This extra dense way of building suggests that there are lower areas that are essentially dark – unless light is reflected in or provided by "light tubes" of the sort that are on the market now. In this model of the first floor with the dark gray representing areas farthest away from natural light we see bright yellow where large skylights let in natural sunshine. There are dark areas using a small amount of artificial light but a minor energy demand compared to the present massively greater use of artificial light at night.

3.6 a Huaibei overall perspective

Huaibei was seeking ideas for its future as its leaders realized it was going to run out of coal, its main industry, in a few short years. In the above drawing I provided a particular idea. Since they are an energy city, and since other cities beat them to taking the lead in wind and solar manufacture on the energy supply side, why not take the lead on the demand side by modeling a city of extreme energy conservation?

Here we see my overall scheme with two keyhole plazas looking toward the lake that has formed due to subsidence from collapsing underground played out coal mines, collapsing and taking suburbs, villages and farm lands with them. (Though they are now harvesting fish where vegetables used to grow…)

3.6 b Huaibei – people, bridges, elevators

People in orange, bridges in pink, exterior elevators in yellow-green. There would be interior elevators too. Because there are linkages above ground level, overall, fewer elevators are needed than in a conventional city.

3.6 c Active and passive solar energy

Active is solar hot water and air and electricity, passive is greenhouses. There is assumed to be a solar electric power plant off picture nearby.

3.6 d Natural, agricultural and ornamental green

3.6 e Arts: gates, sculptures, steps, windows, balconies, walls

3.6 e (2) Zooming in on the arts features image, above

3.6 f Huaibei steps cross section

3.6 g View from Huaibei steps

3.6 h Architects' clusters, gates and views (caption next page)

For some design coherence, clusters and "gates" or openings with special views could be designed by particular architects. Yet the overall city would have architectural variety since a number of architects would participate in the designing of sections of the city. Here we have engaged eleven architects.

3.6.i Views celebrated through the openings of the keyhole plazas

Blue and green views look out on the lake. Yellow looks out toward a nearby mountain. A railroad line is near the top undulating slightly from the horizontal. A small road comes in from the right, ending in a small parking lot; cars and trucks greatly discouraged.

3.7 Village and town for the "Future of Cities" Conference

This drawing was commissioned by ICLEI – Local Governments for Sustainability for their international Future of Cities Conference in Incheon, Korea, 2010. It was used as the backdrop for the stage.

You are beginning to get used to the various features so other than pointing out that there are three levels for pedestrian and bicycle circulation above ground level as well as at ground level, and a street car making loops through the structure also at ground level, what are the tanks on the roof? Water tanks of the sort we see in older New York City pictures, still a few up. In Kathmandu there are many hundreds of them on rooftops providing fresh water under pressure to the buildings below them. Solar heated hot water tanks are also on rooftops and terraces there. Architects hate the raw look (don't remind them of the Pompidou Center in Paris…) and usually erect screening walls to hide them. But these tanks are the low-cost lifeblood of some communities. So in this drawing I have celebrated them painting two of them red. Someone owning the far tank has tried a patterned treatment. The solar electric power plant for this city is at the far right edge of the drawing, a small village to the left, also with its keyhole plaza.

3.8 Semi-dry region town at night

This image I drew largely just to enjoy the colors. It is imagined as a warm climate town in a grasslands area with enough nearby water to celebrate local farming with some on the upper surfaces. No glare from street lights and no obscuring smog from cars so millions of stars come out at night.

4.

Ecocity mapping – ecotropolis to ecovillage

In my books I present a way of looking at city-building I call "the builder's sequence." That means you don't just dump building materials on the construction site and randomly start nailing shingles to plywood. You start with a layout and plan and follow a sequence of steps to rise up from the pattern on the ground, through the building of the foundation and thence up further with walls, roof, floors, and so on until completion of the building. Miss steps in the sequence and expect the mess. You might wish to hang the building in air, but it works from the bottom up. Some "visionary" architects like to defy gravity or use building material off the charts in strength, or imagine anti-gravity building materials but that's not helpful. Deference to reality and a commitment to mastery of challenges with real knowledge and skill are needed for the kind of drawings I imagine leading to built projects, not magic or truly unlikely technologies.

If we are to have ecologically healthy cities, we will need to "roll back sprawl." That's basic, and starts the sequence right from the bottom anchored in the soil. The "ecocity mapping system" shows where and hints at how to layout a city that actually works for extreme low energy, high civility functioning.

We are tending, using this mapping system in the next few pages, to replace the "agglomeration" of city centers, district centers, neighborhood centers and sprawling paving and car suburbs everywhere in many of our metropolitan areas, with something else. That something else would be ecocities, ecotowns and ecovillages we could then call an ecotropolis. The whole ensemble would see nature and agriculture interlaced between the centers with natural waterways and habitat, farm and productive forests returning close in and between the new ecocommunities. New zoning and dedication to a healthy future can adjust our built environments in this direction, gracing and not abusing our bioregions and restoring biodiversity and healthy patterns of evolution.

4.1 a Ecocity map, working copy for Berkeley

My first ecocity map, 1983, was for Berkeley, California. The idea was to indicate the direction of shifting density and diversity of development toward compact pedestrian centers. The purple-pink areas are highest density and the greens are areas where development would be removed for restored open space: opening and restoring waterways, natural habitat, farm production, ridgelines with great view, etc. resulting in energy conservation and ever more pleasant pedestrian areas in the built up areas and highest local biodiversity.

The big downtown is almost dead center in the map, with two major sub-centers in the west and south. Other smaller neighborhood centers see more development and are, in their centers, closer to the new open space of green. The oblong centers in the upper right are that way because they are on a ridge that runs lengthwise through them, that shape on the map reducing the amount of up and down for walking and bicycling in those two neighborhood centers.

Only 28 years later did it dawn on me that this pattern was the beginning of understanding what I decided to call an "ecotropolis," in this case part of the San Francisco Bay Area Ecotropolis.

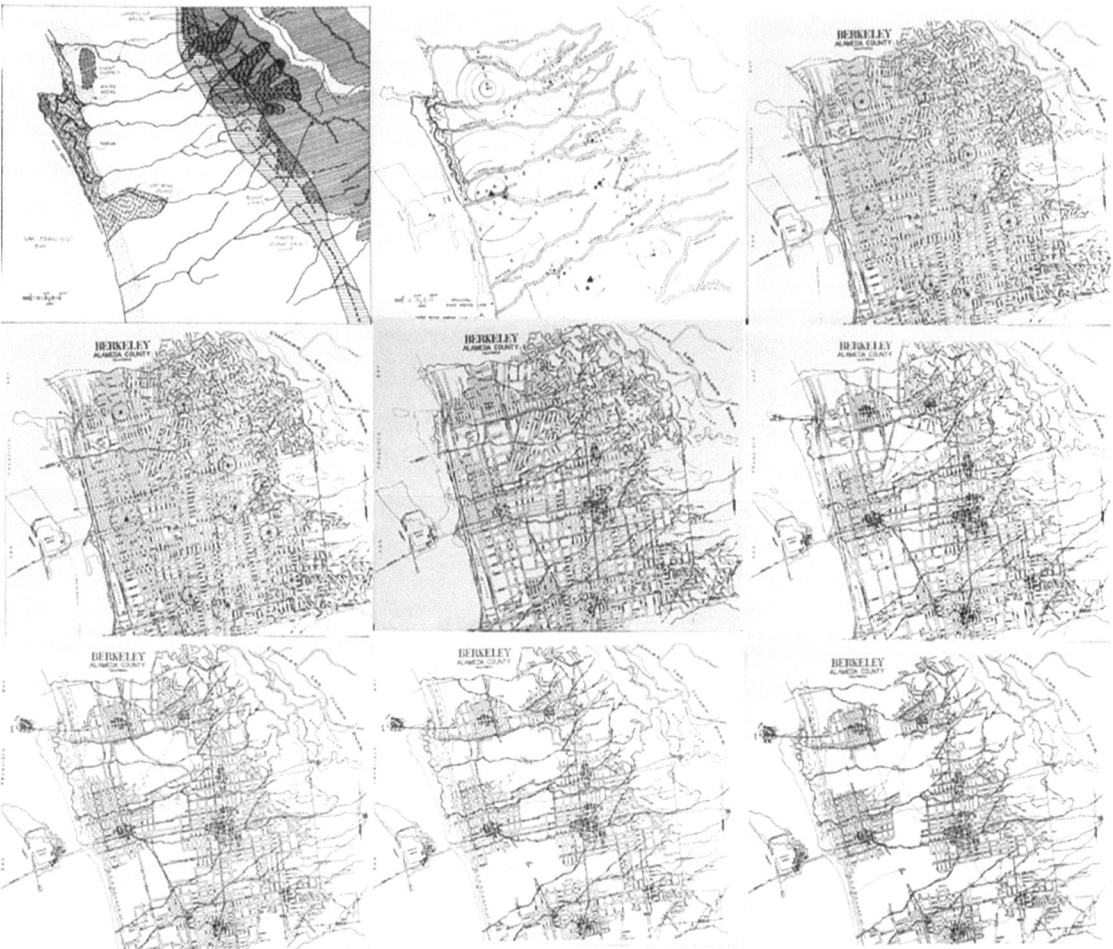

4.1 b Applying the ecocity map over time

My guess is an open-minded, imaginative and committed city could shift its pattern of development in this manner over about 75 to 150 years. If the rule is that existing massively consuming cities are completely resistant to change, there will be a likely collapse of civilization. That important is the form of the city and its design on climate and resources, biodiversity and creativity of its people.

Upper left is the minimally managed "natural" landscape of the native peoples and plants and animals before the whites arrived. Hundred year flood zones, severe earthquake zone, steep slops, landslide and small waterways are shown. Currently the built environment of the city covers almost the entire area of the city with 85% of the creek courses underground in concrete pipes.

In the rest of the maps we see the transition in steps we could expect with shifting zoning leading to shifting actual infrastructure. The darker areas in the centers represent the building of the more dense centers and the white paper opening up represents the return of farming and native plants and animals, waterways and associated educational opportunities for our children – and everyone else as well.

4.2 a Metropolis: NASA satellite photo of the San Francisco Bay Area

This is the only image in this book that I haven't touched. Gray areas are city development.

4.2 b Getting close to ecotropolis: centers located

City, major district and neighborhood centers I've placed roughly where the centers in those scales are located. This image is to create a general understanding of the process that needs great detail in being worked out. These centers in red and orange are the areas receiving the new development that add to population and variety of functions at the same time.

4.2 c Ecotropolis – nature and agriculture return, water rises

At the same time we are turning downtowns, district centers and neighborhood centers into ecocities, ecotowns and ecovillages, we are gradually but resolutely removing sprawl development and developing new farm and nature areas. We also see in this image the bay swelling upwards and spreading over a larger area as even with best ecocity efforts and all the other technologies and life styles that fit, we are slowing climate change. We are likely to see a rise of about two feet give or take some. We don't know what will happen.

4.3 Roll back sprawl

A closer look at removing one and two story development gaining a natural and agricultural landscape with neighborhood centers turning into small hamlets and villages while downtown grows. This imagined for a Berkeley-like landscape.

4.4 Transferring density

Zooming in even closer we see nine houses that used to stand over a buried creek replaced by twelve units of apartments.

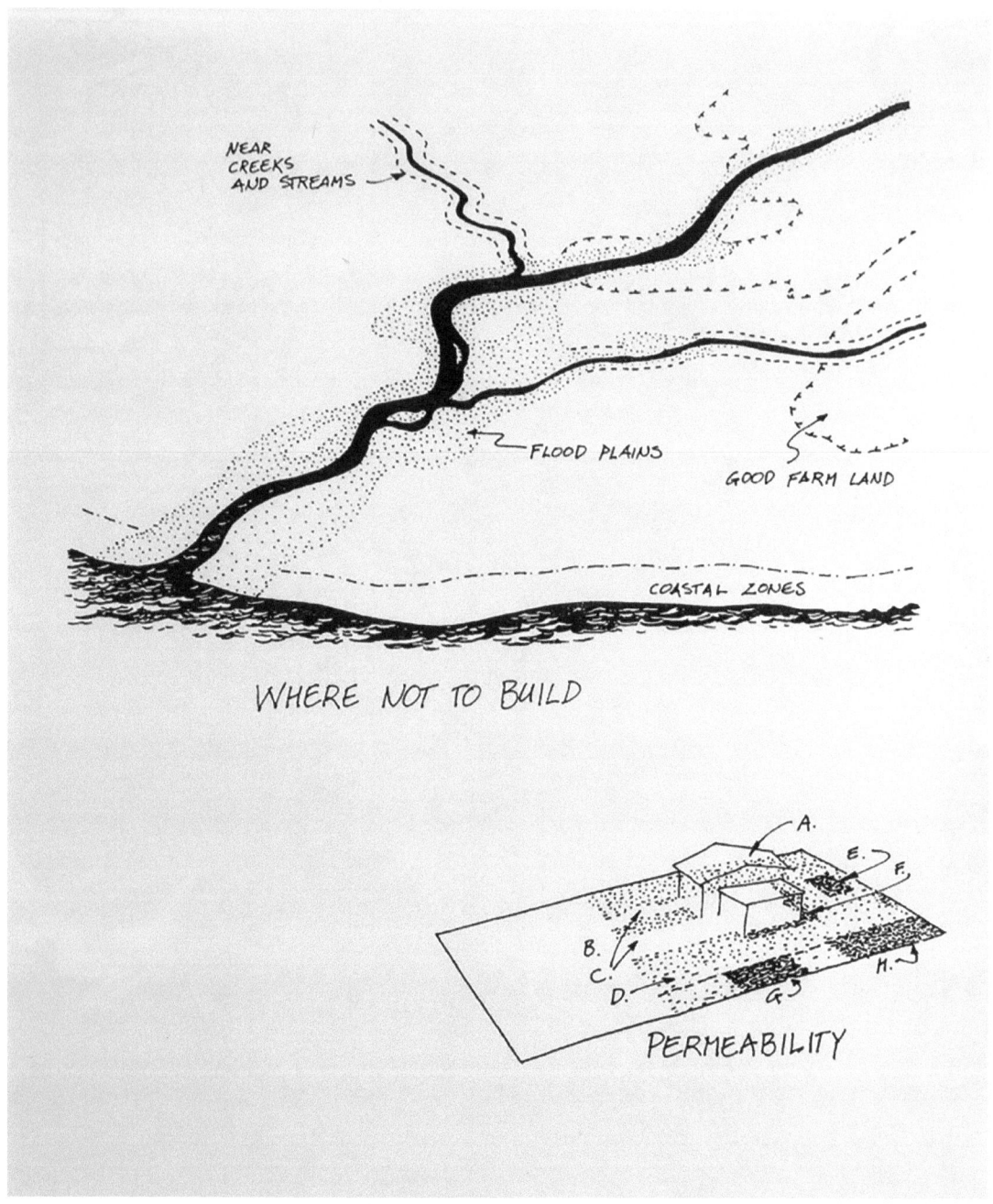

4.5 Where not to build

In general these are areas where it is best not to build, or where building requires higher investment. High enough density and overriding other considerations may indicate that we should build in certain places anyway, such as valuable port space or for extraordinary views. Along coasts or on flood plains, if you must build, build on well compacted artificial elevated earthen mounds to avoid flooding. Fits perfectly with ecocity density and density makes inexpensive per person the cost for elevating the development.

4.6 a Suburb in foreground, distant small town center changing

Here we have three drawings showing a transition from the sort of smaller city chaotic suburban one lot at a time development with a distant town center in the background turning into an ecocity in a pattern you are beginning to become familiar with.

4.6 b Shifting to ecocity and open space, 30 years later

4.6 c Shifting to ecocity and open space, 75 years later

4.7 a A DMZ town, expanded nature (Demilitarized Zone, Korea)

    I attended a conference at a large watch post on the DMZ's south side to assess the future of the DMZ, should peace break out between the North and South. Environmentalists wanted to keep the DMZ completely free of development, developers wanted the whole thing. The dark green band above, about a mile and a half wide, is the DMZ. I proposed that it would be OK to build partially on the DMZ someday if even more space were dedicated to a no-human zone, which is the light green in both this above and the map on the next page. Such a project could assume a leadership role suggesting development everywhere should be dedicated to bringing back nature at the same time as helping people.

4.7 b A DMZ town, on coast line

The same idea but for the east coast where the DMZ meets the ocean.

5.

Arcologies

When I first met Paolo Soleri in 1965 I thought he had hit upon some very important truths: 1. That cities as complex living organisms need to be compact, "mixed use" and essentially three-dimensional – not flat, that is, two-dimensional. They needed to be organized something like complex living organisms which I later thought of as the "anatomy analogy." And… 2. That cities, if in that form, fit beautifully in the natural evolution of life and consciousness in the universe. Relative to both those points Soleri noted that the scattered city of small buildings and vehicles – single family houses instead of apartments, and cars instead of bicycles, buses and trains and elevators – actually constitute by far the larger more wasteful and damaging infrastructure than the compact town designed for people on foot, on bike, and in elevator.

Certain rules of organization therefore pertain, and though I don't strongly advocate Paolo's strictly single structure city concept, I think examples of them should be built as a very high priority human endeavor – they would be something like modern versions of the Southwest Indian pueblo. We'd learn much. Moreover I believe the very compact city of some design, including some of his, also by other individuals, by committees and through democratic charrette processes is a very important component of a future that makes sense. The basic concept has the potential of co-evolutionary success. The present car city, of course, is already causing planetary catastrophe.

Soleri calls his idea "arcology," meaning architecture and ecology brought into an intimate wholeness. A particular kind of ecocity, then, can be "an arcology." I have a few here.

5.1 Zoom through prairie town

Here represented in a sketch from about 1976 we are driving down the highway in, say, Kansas and see an island of civilization in the distance. Relative to its vast open spaces it is really quiet small. And we hurtle through in a matter of seconds.

5.2 Hot climate city by night – to catch the breeze

This small city is set in a very hot climate cooled by the trade winds and the shade of rooftop trees. The city leans into the prevailing breezes like a wave going against the flow, acting as a funnel to draw the cool air through. Nighttime with a distant thunder storm. Without scattered streetlights and air pollution from cars we have stars at night.

5.3 a Tableland

Another one of my favorite drawings. Here we see a person standing on the platform six stories up and another climbing the long, long ladder to the second level. As an abstraction of the three-dimensional principle involved, the image could hardly, I believe, be more elegant.

5.3 b Tableland with built community

Filling out the general notion with living infrastructure. Maybe windmills would pump the water upward. Maybe enough soil could be placed high in the air on the platforms, thick enough to hold the rain and slowly let it drain in small steady streams if the climate there delivered enough precipitation. Rain water collected in elevated cisterns or pumped from lower levels could be released during hours when people could enjoy small waterfalls. Such water flow could also refresh fishponds along its way.

5.4 View from a "sky lobby"

This is a drawing I did for the book *Vertical City – A Solution for Sustainable living* in Chinese and English published by Kenneth King and Kellogg Wong. It is rather fanciful with a twisted perspective for viewing a small area at a time while scanning. Among several ideas here is using fossil "fuels" as biological origin resources to create architectural grade thick, hard plastics such as the transparent awning and the skylight we see lower center with bicycles passing over. The thin struts holding up the highest level would be expensive extra strong striated steel. Expensive as conventional structural materials go but cheap compared to the expensiveness of much automobile infrastructure.

In this case we are looking out from a sky lobby, a busy landing for several elevators at about the 12th floor level.

5.5 a   Three climates Arcologies – temperate

In this set of four pedestal and bridge linked structures we have not quite a single structure city but almost. We are adapting the basic structure to local climate and sunshine circumstances.

This is the mid-latitudes version of the basic design with some passive heating in relating to the sun angles. We are here looking north, the structures collecting a fair amount of warming energy from the sun and by virtue of their compactness, energy conserving in terms of sharing heating and cooling energy by way of sharing walls and ceilings/floors.

5.5 b Hot climate – shade structures

In the low latitudes, between the equator and the Tropic of Cancer and Tropic of Capricorn, heat rather than cold is the problem. Here we see shade structures that double as surfaces for various activities, one in this illustration as a link between three separate structures. Plus there are bridges and terraces that link. The shade from the horizontal "flanges" shall we call them, also helps cool the entire structure. The mass tends to stay close to the temperature of the soil beneath as in the "Shaban effect" mentioned earlier, illustration 1.9.

5.5 c Cold climate, heavy on the solar greenhouses

In a really cold climate, but with a fair amount of sunshine, we might see the same overall design like this but with strong emphasis on sun-facing solar greenhouses and upper level wind screens.

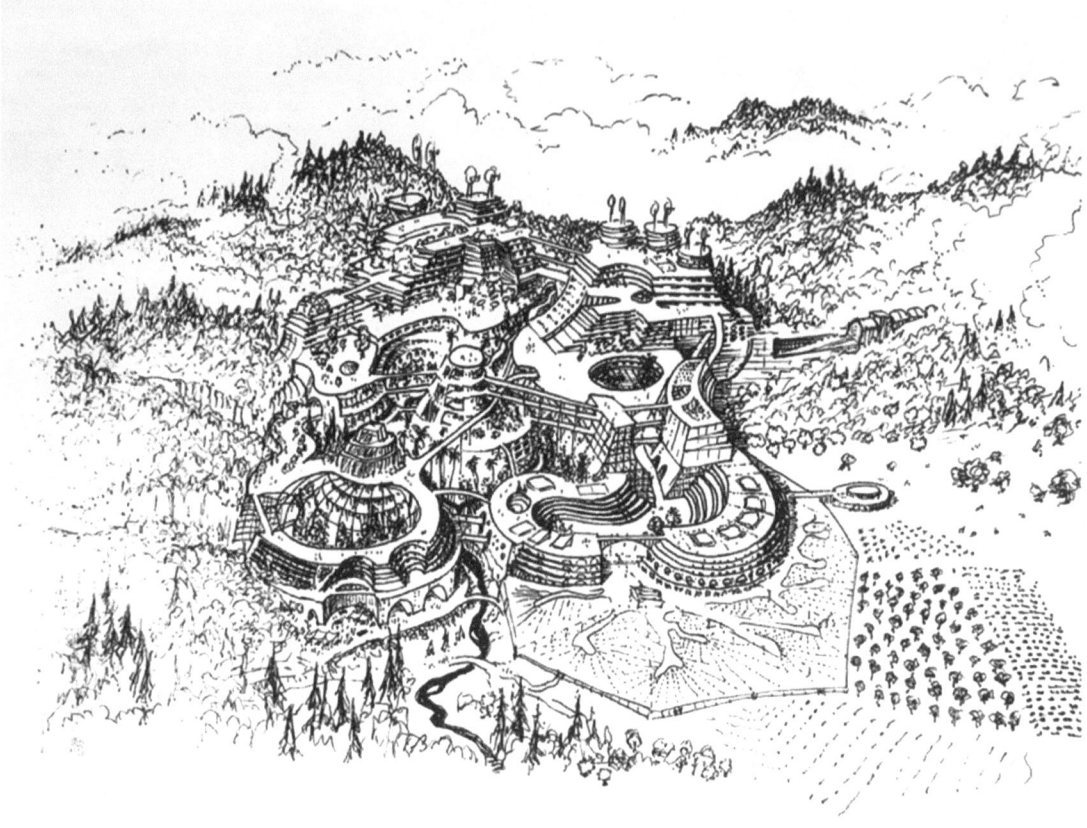

5.6 Semi-arcology, Santa Cruz

This design is getting close to an arcology of the sort Soleri might produce but a little more scattered out, still functioning at very high levels of efficiency. We imagine here that two small streams are arriving at a confluence just before leaving town as a larger single stream, picture center.

Imagine the government for the collective good, instead of building massive highway infrastructure with freeways, cloverleaf intersections, parking structures and much if not most of law enforcement dedicated simply to traffic management, simply provided the free basic structure – freeplace instead of freeway. An ecocity skeleton, or call it shelf system, could be provided to ecocity developers as government pays for car infrastructure benefiting sprawl developers today. Imagine here that each plane you see was three stories from the one below and individual or the developer could build mixed-use structures between the slabs of concrete and steel in any way they thought might be ecologically healthy and that fit health standards and safety codes.

I did this drawing thinking of the environment north of Santa Cruz, California with orchards, vineyards and forest producing wood, mushrooms, pine nuts, medicinal and other products as major components of the economy. In the upper right, a train station to points over the hill and across California and the United States, Canada, Mexico…

5.7 Town as hill, Gene Zellmer inspired

Zellmer, a California architect dreamed up this arcology-like design, which I improvised on. The exterior apartments and condominiums face out over natural and food producing landscapes. Their inward "front" doors connect with the location of offices, jobs, manufacturing, meeting places, hotels and the like. The roof has playgrounds, restaurants, big skylights and swimming pool.

6.

Fractals

We in the ecocity tradition have called the notion of the truly complete ecocity project in an existing city an "integral project" or "integral area" since around 1975. Around 2003 architect and ecocity designer Paul Downton of Adelaide, Australia suggested the term "ecocity fractal." A fractal is a fraction of the whole, in this case a whole ecocity, with all essential and mutually supportive parts and functions present and well arranged. So ecocity fractal and integral project are one and the same thing.

In my travels speaking in 35 countries to date and visiting a total of several more I have neither found a "full spectrum" ecocity nor a "piece of an ecocity" with all parts present much less well arranged as well. I've never seen a complete living ecocity organism, whether the whole item or some smaller complete example of the fractal sort. The smaller part, of course, is far more easily, inexpensively and quickly built than a whole new city, whether from fresh cloth on previously undeveloped land or by way of transforming part of an existing city. But if built, even a small "fractal" would be a powerful and I believe very comprehensible means to understand and promote ecocities.

Tianjin Eco-city is under construction as I write and I've visited five times. They credit me with their name so I'm very happy about that. It is a whole new city approach. It has many excellent technologies, restoration projects for wildlife and a network of bicycle and footpaths. Not bad, a start. But it also has oversized streets and blocks that tempt automobile use and speeding, lacks many of the design features I provide in this book and is missing such unifying layouts and massing designs suggested here such as "keyhole plazas." Given this as one of the really exemplary projects on the planet today, and knowing it is still not complete in the ecocity sense is an added incentive to move forward with a genuinely complete, full bodied ecocity project on a small scale: a fractal.

6.1 Integral neighborhood for West Berkeley, 1976 proposal

Around 1976 I proposed an "integral project" for the west side of Berkeley, California where I was living just seven or eight blocks away. There was a largely open space on two blocks there awaiting some sort of development. This was a design I proposed that wasn't built. In the zoom in we can see pedestrian streets – larger blue arrows – leading into interior areas. On the fourth level (fifth in some areas) we see an interlinked floor that has a restaurant and café, shops of a good variety and a small rooftop garden. The area was traditionally highly mixed use, including small manufacture. Red outlined deck on the second level is private, dark and light green on the fourth level is a shared community space and garden and the restaurant, café, shops and garden level above that outlined in brown. Smaller blue arrows show narrow pedestrian passages into the development.

6.2 A step on the way: work-live, multi-family country house

In this design we have about as small an "integral" of the larger ecocity that we could imagine. This is even much smaller than ecovillages. This structure serves as a group house for three families sharing several facilities in the co-housing model.

6.3 Almost a fractal

Imagined for a town center with creek restored, we have here above a project that respects the sun angles, the natural creek, and that accommodates housing, offices and shops. A covered street mid-block, sometimes called a galleria, adds to the pedestrian convenience. It was imagined for Berkeley, California across from the Act II movie theater, now gone, with design elements reflecting a popular hotel.

6.4 Big block downtown fractal with grand hallway

Looking in more closely than we did in illustrations 1.5a and 1.5b, pages 17 and 18, we have here a tall integral project or ecocity fractal created from four urban blocks. In the upper right we see through one of the great halls that intersect, formerly a street for cars.

6.5 Town of bridge-linked fractals

As keyhole plazas could be collected into a total pedestrian design, illustrations 3.5a through 3.5c, pages 41 through 43, so a whole ecocity could be made of linked ecocity fractals like highly mixed use pyramids – linking tightly integrated clusters of essentially joined structures on ground level and by bridges. Here an enormous flock of migratory birds swirls through town.

6.6 a. Heart of the City Project designs for downtown Berkeley

I proposed a number of designs for a project for downtown Berkeley that involved the possibility of opening Strawberry Creek, the city's central water way that is buried through most of its course from its springs in the Berkeley Hills to San Francisco Bay. Here is one version of the integral project, based on a photograph of the downtown, with the creek running through the right central portion of the drawing.

6.6 b. The same site and variety of functions, extra modern

A modern 1950s version might look something like this, still with exactly the same mix of uses and multiplicity of functions together in a design respecting sun angles and accommodating work, live, solar active and passive, rooftop activities, small public plaza, elevated gardens and so on, in addition to opening the creek.

6.6 c. The same site with favorite Arts and Crafts style

Berkeley Architecture Heritage Association likes Arts and Crafts and so-called Berkeley Brown Shingle styles. The same functions as the earlier two drawings prevail here but with a very different look.

6.6 d. The same site, again, with usual city variety

Another composite of different styles common in Berkeley could turn out a design that looks like this. The design here unites most of two blocks with a bridge building and involves two streets transformed into pedestrian areas, one with the creek opening project. In the background are the Berkeley Hills and the University of California campus with its nearly 300 foot tall Venice-like Campanile.

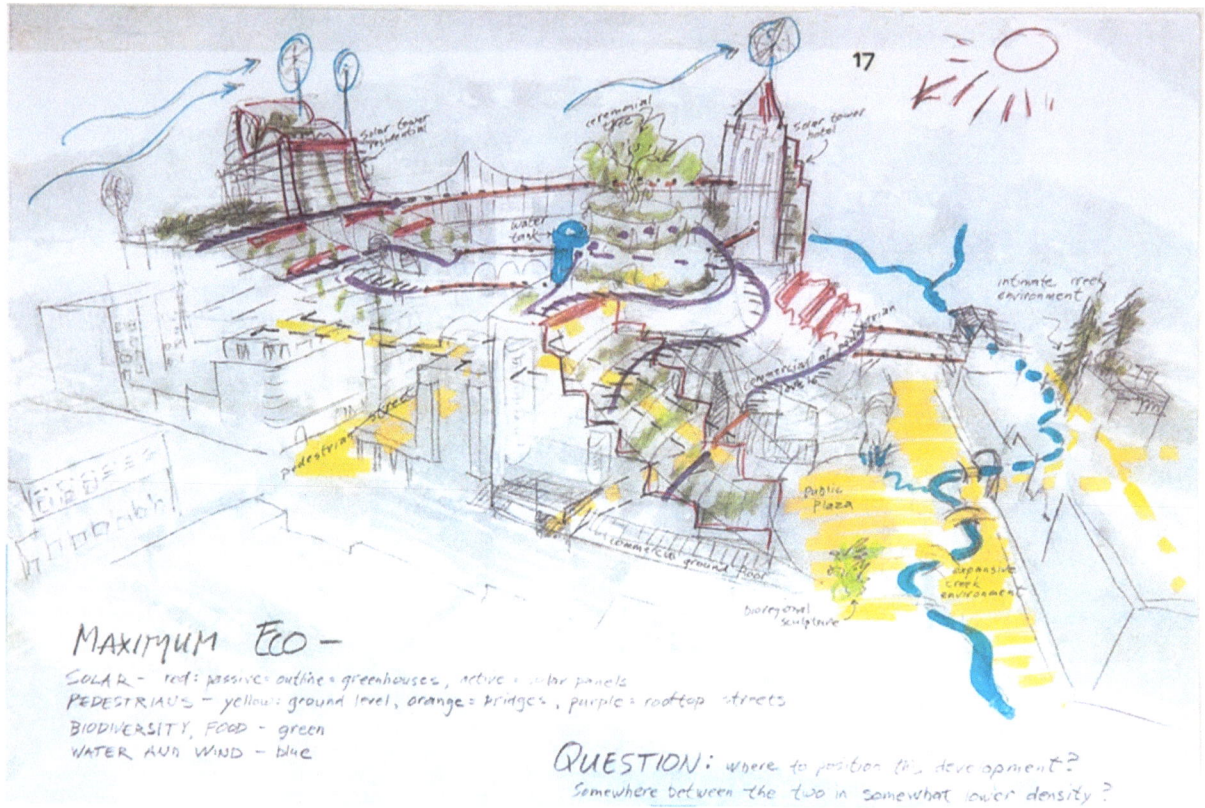

6.6 e. Circulation: bridges, ground level, rooftops, water

Sketch of various functions in another version yet. Red for passive solar angles utilized to help warm the integral project. Yellow for ground level public open space and passages through the two blocks in question. Blue: water tank, creek with fountain to the left of the creek and draining into it and for water pumping wind machines to raise water into high places, green for some of the planting on terraces. Purple for walkways on two elevated levels. And red-orange for several bridges.

6.6 f. Addison St. bridge building, Heart of the City Project

Between the two blocks in consideration here runs Addison Street and in this design a bridge building crosses the street, bollards turning it into a pedestrian street under the bridge. Here is one of the large rooftop trees, essentially an eco-art element attracting native birds.

6.6 g. Sixth Floor Street Café, Heart of the City Project

A café overlooking the city center of San Francisco, the Golden Gate Bridge and distant Pacific Ocean. Here we see a Cal student studying for a class, railing left out for a better view.

6.7 a. and b. Implantations added to a city

"Implantation" is architect Herb Greene's term for an architectural element set into an existing city or town infrastructure, but here in this case, a very dense ecocity fractal inserted into a city with buildings around 15 stories high. The largest implant, below, rises about 45 stories, complete with shade structures, being in a hot climate, and continuous green plants and ecological regime of birds, insects – maybe lizards and frogs? – spiraling up to the top floors. The continuous green integral environment is championed by architect Ken Yeang, of Malaysia.

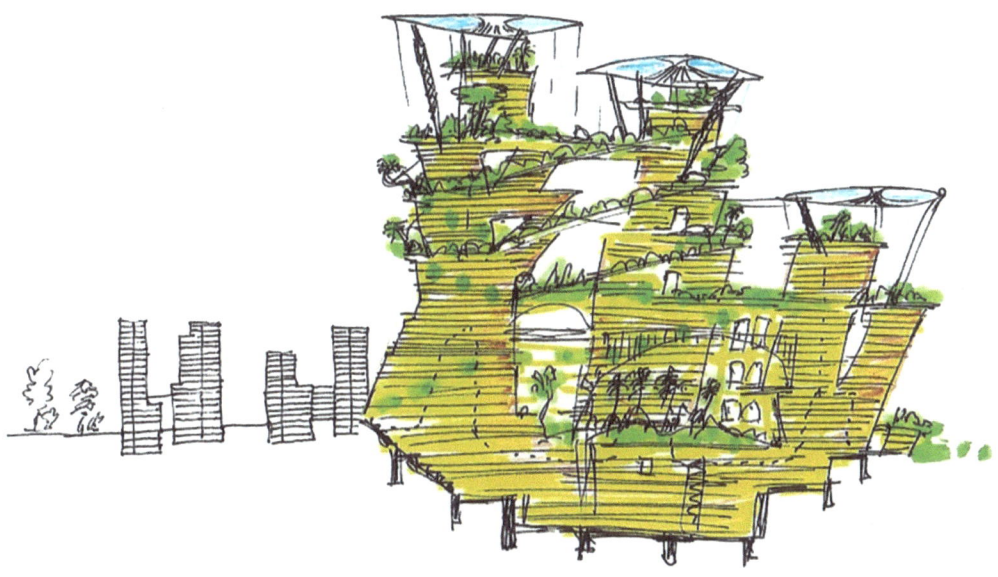

6.8 a. Implantation with subway train leaving the center

I drew this image for a report for Tianjin Eco-city, China, suggesting an ecocity fractal implantation schematically represented for the kind of blocky city structure of relatively large buildings – the on-edge rectangular boxes you see here – typical in China's new development. The idea is for yet higher density but lively, quiet interiors something like a cross between a system of plazas and streets lit dramatically by large skylights.

Here we imagine, say, the functions provided for by ten of the big box buildings are taken up in the volume of the new structure inset into what would otherwise be a uniform pattern of big boxes. The open space gained, lower left, minus the removed building indicated by the dashed lines, can be for park, plaza, food gardening or natural environment, plus there is shelter for many more people and activities.

7.

Downtowns

Downtowns are a particularly rich economic and cultural opportunity for an ecocity fractal or development headed in that direction, in fact, a whole intense ecocity, yet just out the door, nature and farm. Steps short of a full fractal or ecocity development can nonetheless be headed in the right direction. A few follow here.

Downtowns are also traditionally the location of most accepted higher density and taller buildings. Thus in downtowns heading in an ecocity direction there is more citizen support for the intensive architecture that explores the outer reaches of ecocity three-dimensional imagination and living. In an odd way, the larger more expensive projects here might lead into the smaller but more dense than current examples of smaller district and neighborhood centers where NIMBY (Not In My Back Yard) and anti-all-kinds-of-development resistance usually dominates. Downton areas could then show that some elements of three-dimensionality could be practical and pleasurable on all scales.

7.1 Berkeley Civic Center Park with creek

Berkeley City Hall from my 1987 book, "Ecocity Berkeley," with then and presently banished Strawberry Creek brought back to rejoin the citizens, taller buildings with rooftop arboretums in the background, fruit orchards in the park, forest of redwoods and a functioning fountain that has been dry for decades.

7.2 Rural town center with stars at night

Another case of starry night made possible by few streetlights, unlike in the suburbs, and no glare from smog because of automobile pollution.

7.3 San Francisco downtown with bridges

One of the rare drawings where I used a ruler. On the rooftop of the second from closest building on the left foreground there is a tennis court and on the side of the stepped up building just beyond the tennis court building is a giant mural of an orchid. Many other of the details you are quite used to by now.

7.4 *San Francisco, quick sketch*

For those who like to see the process of developing images and ideas, this is the first quick sketch on scratch paper leading toward the drawing I most commonly use rather generically for Ecocity Builders website and other "branding."

7.5 San Francisco – a more developed pen and ink drawing

7.6 Small downtown creek environment

    We can imagine small waterways becoming central features in lively downtowns, lending a little calm in their midst. Creek courses should be deep enough to accommodate floods – and keep the citizens informed about the realities of nature – like the power of flowing water. Such features are especially important for educating the children, who love creeks in any case. (Landscape architects generally hate somewhat deeper "canyons" for waterways in designed urban environments and instead like to create "water features" at a very high level as near sidewalk and street grade as possible. They like a planned, mechanical, steady supply of water for their one mode environments that look like theirs not nature's creation. Meantime storm water is shunted off into oversized underground flood water pipes.) High water events are very exciting for children and the youthfulness in almost everyone (except landscape architects it seems). In this image larger floods cover the paths down from sidewalk level and rise to the level of the base of the big tree on the left – then the creek spends the other 95% of its time looking pretty much as illustrated here.

7.7 Downtown market with shade cloth and rooftop trees

A simple way to cool streets in hot climates or during hot days is to use cloth stretched over public open space as in the case of this market place scene here. I've added admittedly rather impractically large rooftop trees but more modest ones make a lot of sense and cast beautiful, rippling soft shadows.

8.

Plazas

Public plazas offer design opportunities that serve and communicate with the citizens in an especially important way, central to the whole city, town or village or to any particular district or neighborhood of a city where located. They can be of almost any size. The extra-large, like Tiananmen Square in Beijing or the Zocalo in Mexico City, are designed for exhibition of high orders of power, wealth and grandeur. They make small and impersonal the human body but even at grand scale offer many opportunities for cultural and economic expression from festivals to marketplaces, from military displays to political rallies and protests – often *against* military displays.

What the ecocity offers, and probably especially to the middle sized and small plazas, is a new set of arrangements that come from celebrating nature and surrounding the plazas with the best of ecological architecture tuned to the local conditions of sun, wind, rain, temperature and cultural tradition. The notion of opening small waterways through plazas and configuring plazas to look out over and frame celebrated views to nature from where the city sits, I believe, is a major contribution to both architecture and city planning. Such plazas further the understanding of what ecocities actually are and how they work. I call such plazas "view plazas" or "keyhole plazas" and have already illustrated them a number of times to this point in this book, I believe one of the best ideas around.

8.1 Arcata, California future plaza, view to hills

The front row of buildings around the central plaza in Arcata, California looks much like this. But in this drawing commissioned by my friend and petroleum analyst turned anti-oil activist, Jan Lundberg, who lived there at the time, I've added a diverted creek, pond, associated birds and the view up to the hills. This view was created by removing a few buildings on the northeast corner. I've added a second row of buildings that rise two to four stories above the front row of two and three story buildings, in other words going to about four to seven stories from street level making the plaza look like it is surrounded by small hills covered with buildings in a locally consistent style. The bird on the President McKinley statue actually landed there while I was sketching my preliminary drawing.

8.2 Elevated keyhole plaza

    This image of an elevated keyhole plaza on the high third floor level over a shopping center is so detailed as to be a little overly chaotic, like many cities are. Zoom in though and it's fun to check out the angles of a kind of birds eye view – or fish eye lens? The large transparent plastic architectural elements are the same idea in this image as in illustration 5.4, page 70, the Sky Lobby from *Vertical City*. Why burn up all our fossil fuels when they could be made into things like these? Part of the floor of the plaza is thick super hard and very clear plastic. Also seen is an awning protecting a balcony walkway on the left and a water-collecting trough like structure leading fresh rainwater to a cistern under the building in the upper right corner of the drawing. As with the large trees high in buildings, these double as a kind of eco-art element in the city.

8.3 Union Square, San Francisco

A drawing for San Francisco Focus Magazine. Presently there's a six story underground parking garage beneath the plaza. I was suggesting the above with a fog making element added to the victory column for the United States' first long distance imperialistic victory – in the Spanish American War.

9.

Transport

Access can be provided by transportation networks and vehicles or by design such that so much variety is close together that no vehicles are needed for personal transportation at all: just walk around the corner and there it is. "Access by proximity" is a kind of formula or slogan I use to encapsulate the idea.

Given foot, bicycle and public transportation. I see no reason to include any cars in the "complete" ecocity at all. There are none in Venice, Italy; Zermatt, Switzerland; Gulongyu, China; Lamu, Kenya and a few other cities today around the world, even almost none in the town of Avalon on the island of Catalina right off the coast of none other than Los Angeles itself, pioneering car capital of the world. I've been asked after a number of my talks if it is even possible to have cities without cars. I've replied that there were cities with no cars for the first 4,500 years of human urban civilization – simply because there were no cars up to a little more than 100 years ago. Somehow our ancestors survived!

A "transportation hierarchy" for a healthy city can be usefully held in mind: design first for the pedestrian including in the higher density areas with bridges between buildings and ground level passageways through larger blocks for high pedestrian permeability and convenience. Next, design for the bicycle, then motorized systems including elevators and rail-based systems like streetcars, metros and city-to-city trains. Last on the list, to fill in gaps, design for busses, but with fixed routes serving centers of development. In the size and function range of today's typical automobile, provide only for emergency vehicles. Trucks, delivery vehicles and firefighting equipment should be accommodated to the urban design, not vice versa. Thus, for example, such vehicles are simply smaller in compact European cities with narrow streets than in the United States. They still do a fine job delivering water and safety services.

9.1 Vegetable Garden Car

Also known as the Vegetable Car, was first this drawing and later a real 360 horse power 1969 Pontiac GTO I turned into a vegetable garden. From 1979 to 1988 it was out and about Berkeley and San Francisco with no engine and registered with the State of California officially as a "trailer." It had wheels though – the one in the picture above didn't.

I was standing in line in Munich, Germany at the train station near midnight and someone tapped me on my shoulder and said, "Didn't I see you watering your Vegetable Car in front of your house in Berkeley last week?" And he had. Another person back in California one day was looking disapprovingly at the Vegetable Car and said, "what if everyone did that to their cars?" I realized then I was getting through to some people.

9.2 Delivery vehicles of the future

Simple solution: slow and low powered for an urban environment, demands very little energy, non-polluting, not dangerous. More that fit below.

9.3 Bike, bus and cart

9.4 Future of the automobile industry – if healthy

Transportation and urban arrangements and design are intimately interrelated and thus cars, if they are not to destroy us, will bifurcate to fit ecocities, splitting into the very small – cart – and the larger physically but smaller per person – streetcar. Car companies should plan to recognize this pattern and remission for the ecocity future producing the carts and streetcars, and also elevators, moving sidewalks for highest density areas, train station accoutrements, fork lifts and other equipment that fits the ecocity. They lobby for tax advantages, seek government military and fleet contracts and influence zoning to promote cars. They could do their usual activities on behalf of transportation, but produce products that actually fit the ecocity and do a good turn for the planet – and stay in business.

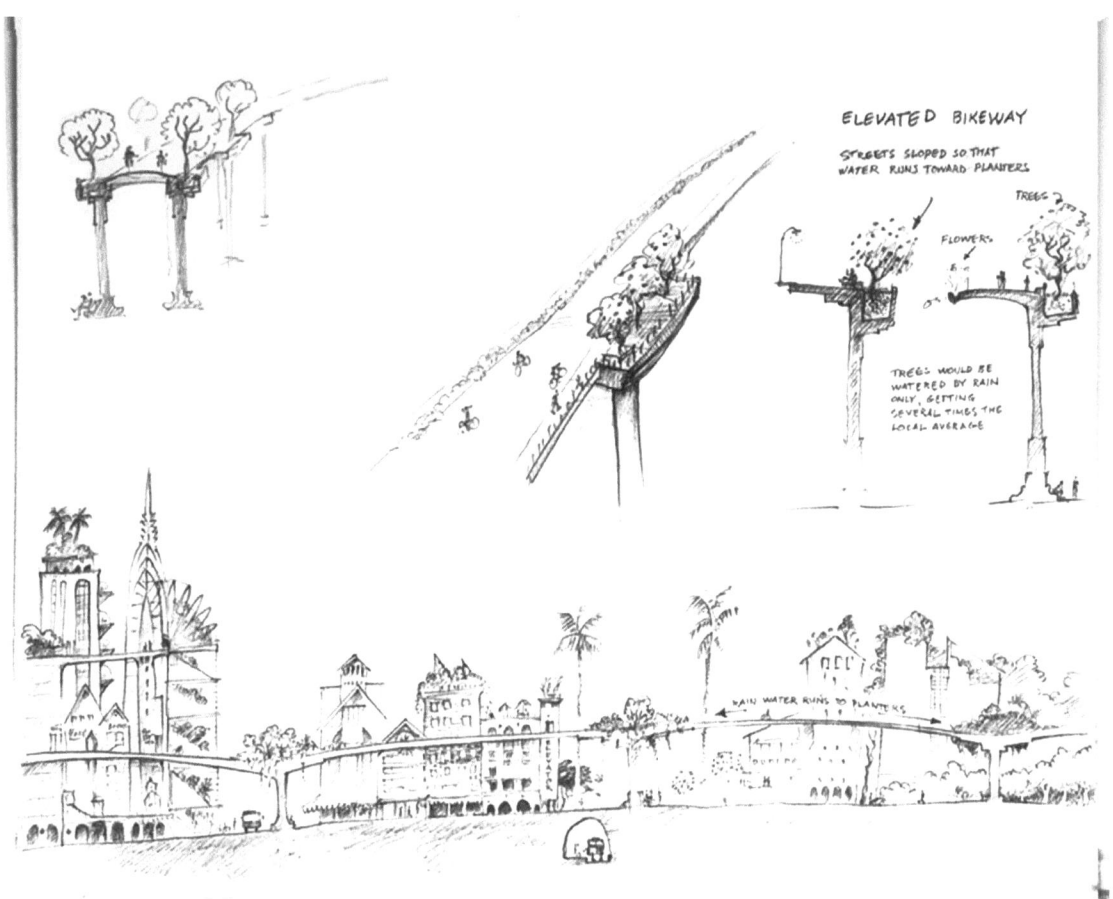

9.4 Elevated bicycle freeway

(Excellent word, psychologically speaking, freeway.) When I drew this picture around 1984 I thought I invented the idea of an elevated bicycle freeway. When doing a random Google search in 2010, which would be 26 years later, looking into the history of the Pasadena freeway where I had my first (not too bad) car crash – not my fault – on the oldest section of freeway in the United States, I discovered there was an elevated bicycle path constructed on that same route called the California Cycleway, a wooden elevated bicycle freeway opened in the year 1900 four decades before the Pasadena Freeway. There are even pictures of it in Wikipedia. The Cycleway went out of business almost immediately. It was supremely unlucky in timing, appearing just as cars were becoming popular and beginning to run bicycles off the streets both literally in fact and in style.

My idea was also to have the elevated cycleway arched slightly so precipitation would flow toward the support columns. They would be arched for strength as well as for natural drainage that would work with certain native plants that would be placed in soil where the collected rainwater would end up in the rainy season.

9.5 Street becomes pedestrian hallway with skylights

Here we coordinate the creation of a pedestrian interior hallway with adding newer development in centers. The dashed line represents the earlier buildings replaced by the larger later ones. The former street is turned into a hallway and is lit dramatically by skylights, and on the smaller scale, by area lights electrically powered and with light tube or fiber optic-delivered sunshine. On cloudy days, part of these interiors are simply a little darker.

9.6 New bridge building helps create a pedestrian street

Same idea as on the previous page in a different design. In this case the old buildings are still there – with stippled "gray" walls, the new white building placed immediately behind the front row of buildings in the foreground.

9.7 Installing plastic bridge between buildings

Here comes more pedestrian friendly transport – using shoes – linking buildings. You will remember the clear plastic structural elements in the elevated keyhole plaza from page 101. Here we use petroleum products to link buildings rather than burning them to power transport, wreck the climate and destroy the coastal homes of one quarter of humanity with rising seas.

I've also shown a sway-reducing shock absorber to use between buildings of different sway periods in earthquakes to buffer one another and reduce the destructive movement.

SISSOR LIFT AND
CHERRY PICKER TOURS

9.8 Flying through town

When your city becomes a place to *really* enjoy: scissor lift and cherry picker rides.

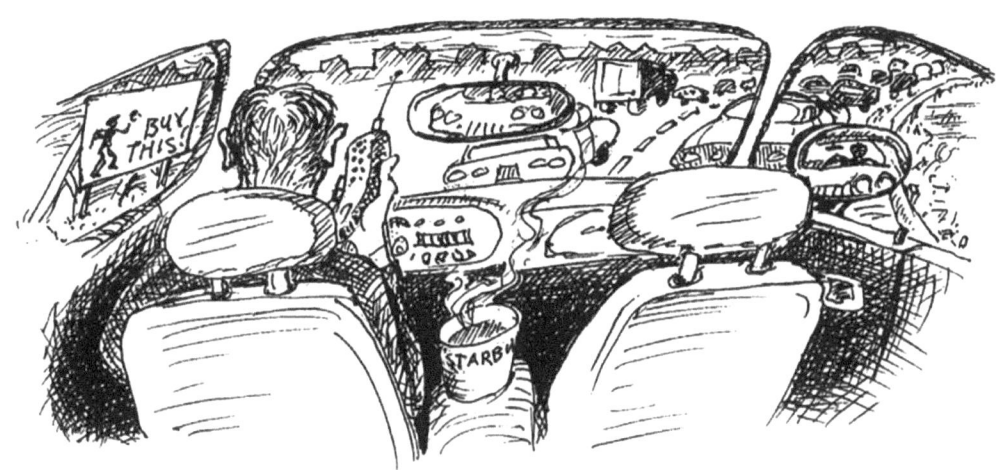

9.9 Car reality again

Divide the time you are stuck in traffic as well as driving in your car, the time waiting for repairs, cleaning and polishing and working to pay for the vehicle, gasoline, crash insurance and repairs, etc. into the distance, covered and you are averaging, in the US, about five miles an hour. Source of those figures: Ivan Illich in his book *Energy and Equity*. It is dated, 1974, but the situation is *worse* now.

10.

Villages

It is important that people understand that more than half the people in the world now live in cities but it is even more important that people understand that more than 95% live in cities, towns and villages and at all those scales the built environment has been disastrously transformed by the automobile. It is the key component that makes the city worse as it, the car, gets better. Los Angeles improved the automobile in the 1960s with the "smog device" rather than improving the city in which the automobile, along with low-density development, paving and a cheap energy supply, are all integrally linked. The result was locally improved air quality, "proof" that the sprawling city of cars could be "improved." The rest of the world's cities and even towns and villages followed. The result: global climate change, accelerated extinctions and biodiversity collapse and other true disasters we have yet to face honestly.

Villages, as well as cities, have been radically damaged by the automobile. Yet in their traditional form, with every opportunity for "access by proximity" because of their small size, they can model whole systems design for neighborhood and small town scale up to downtown and whole city scale. In many ways, understanding the built environment as appropriately laid out in the soil and on the surface of the planet is as important as things get, and thus the best of villages is crucially needed in this age that claims to be "urban."

10.1 Ecotopian ecovillage on a bay in Northern California

I always think of this illustration as looking like one of the towns in my friend Earnest – "Chick" to his friends – Callenbach's book "Ecotopia," an entertaining and enlightening mix between a novel and a city planning tract for ecocities. The book, half of it, reports back to New York City about the newly created country of Ecotopia that seceded from the U.S. when the Motherland was distracted in one of its perpetually cycling oil wars, while those back to nature types from Northern California, Oregon and Washington dropped out of the nation state and set up their car-free world. The other half of the book is the personal life of our hero, against his somewhat cynical nature, falling in love with the place and of course an Ecotopian woman. The above is an illustration I did for a benefit talk Chick once gave for my ecocity organization. On the pier that is a giant salmon and a sturgeon, native to the San Francisco region, being carried toward banquet dinners.

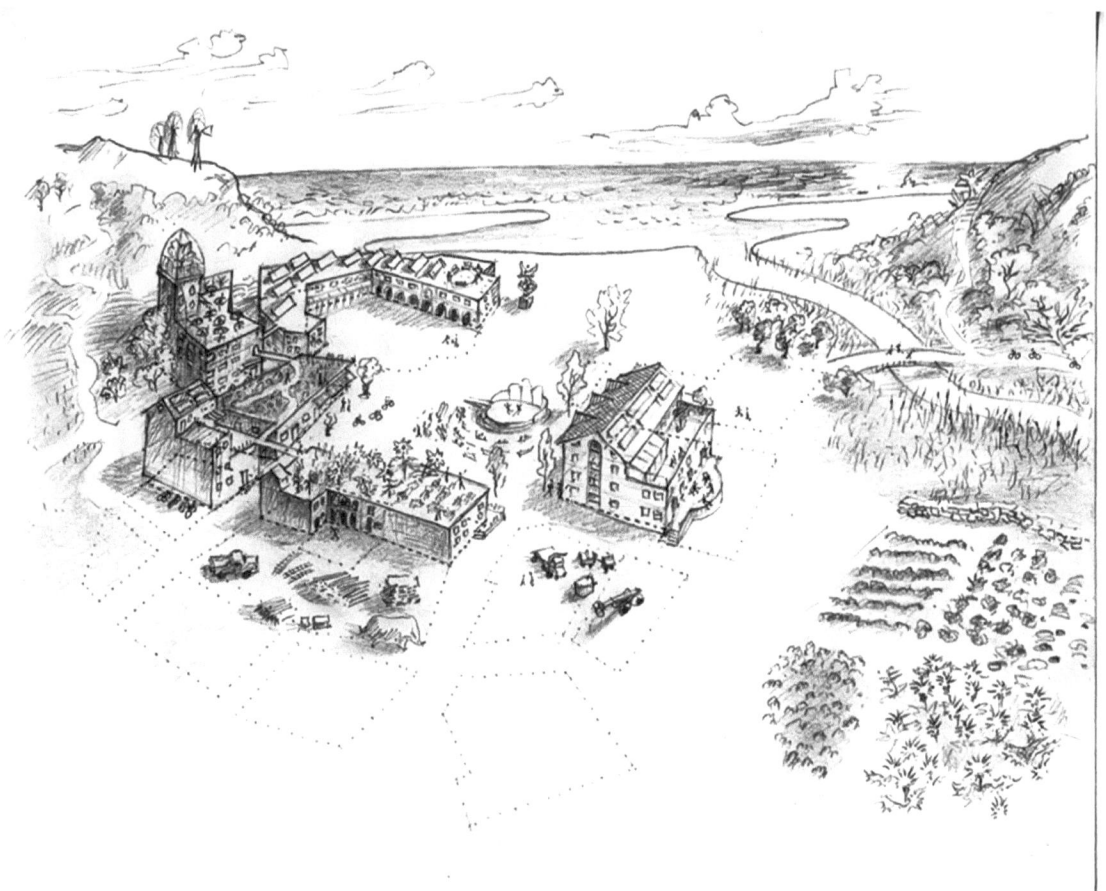

10.2a Village, beginnings

Dotted lines represent locations of future buildings.

10.2 b Village grows, here portrayed as an X-ray image

The village on previous page, illustration 10.2 a "finished out." I give this the strange name X-ray Village because we can see through the far sides of the buildings to the street front sides of the buildings behind so that their design and the layout of the streets can be viewed.

This represents another technique in attempting to visualize and communicate such as those mentioned in Chapter 2. Adding color adds definition of surfaces and makes various things stand out that are missed with gray only imagery.

10.3 a Bicycle City

This village series was drawn for a client wanting to build a Bicycle City. The location he wanted to keep confidential. But the rail line is actually there and the site is a bike-able distance from a nearby lively town. Cartoonist Marc Nugi turned this image into a movie with wind mills turning, train zipping by, dancers dancing on the stage, sun reflecting off the solar collectors, bicyclist and dog walker bicycling and dog walking, beaver swimming and diving, gardener hoeing and garden vegetables and trees moving in the wind.

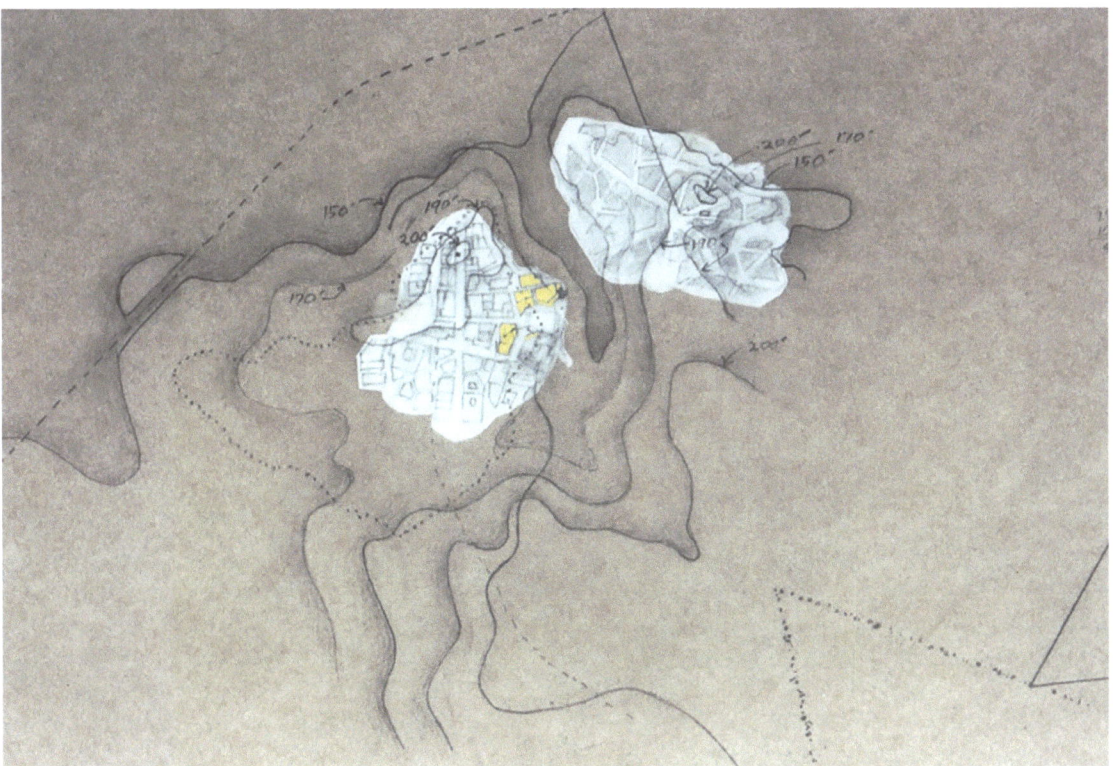

10.3 b Sketchy Bicycle City topography map and rough layout

Looking down at the generalized contours of the landscape for Bicycle City. Hoping to be a low budget start up, the first buildings, in yellow, were to be built while enthusiasm and investment also built up – for later expansion among future lovers of bicycles and living close to nature.

10.3 c Bicycle City's first structures

Zooming in on the topo map we see the first structures that could be built with the limited capital available for the project. Four buildings and a wall define a rudimentary keyhole plaza with a view down into and across a small valley. The perspective also takes a glancing view to the edge of a future cluster of buildings and streets, next large phase of the long-term project. You can also see the planned street system of the first of the twin settlements, assuming sufficient funds. These streets, some quite narrow and all designed for pedestrians and cyclists are to the left of the original four buildings and wall. The wall is a built feature to define limits of the eventual plaza open space and to heighten the sense of the keyhole plaza view even before a building is constructed there to replace the wall.

One feature I'm especially fond of is the "T" intersection defined by the three buildings on the upper, or north, side of the plaza. I could imagine finding myself standing there and feeling like I'm in the middle of an intersection almost completely lost in an urban street scene but with the natural environment only one block away.

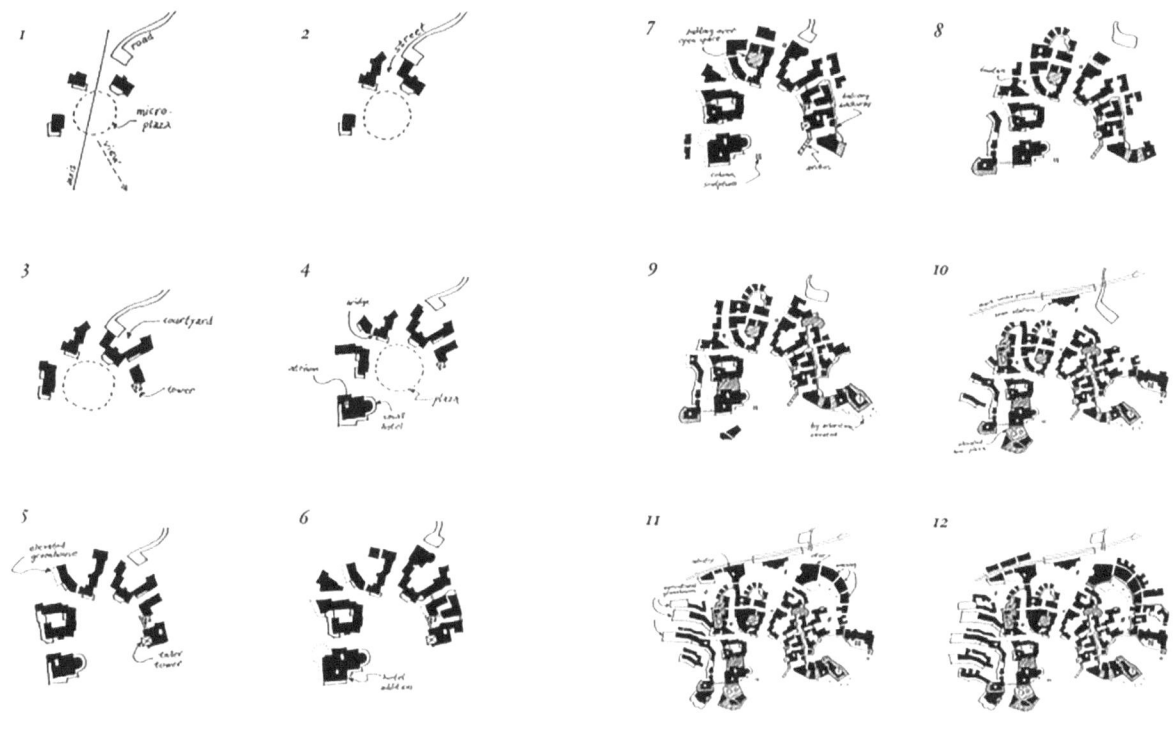

10.4 a Growing futuristic ecovillage maps

This drawing I have to admit is a little too fine detailed for a book format, but you get the idea. This small beginning grows into a large village in the course of, say, 50 years. You will recognize the courtyards, plazas and irregular streets. By stage 10 above, in its development, a small train station is added.

The technique here, appropriate to Chapter 2, is that the scale of the map gradually shrinks as we progress from the 1st image to the 12th.

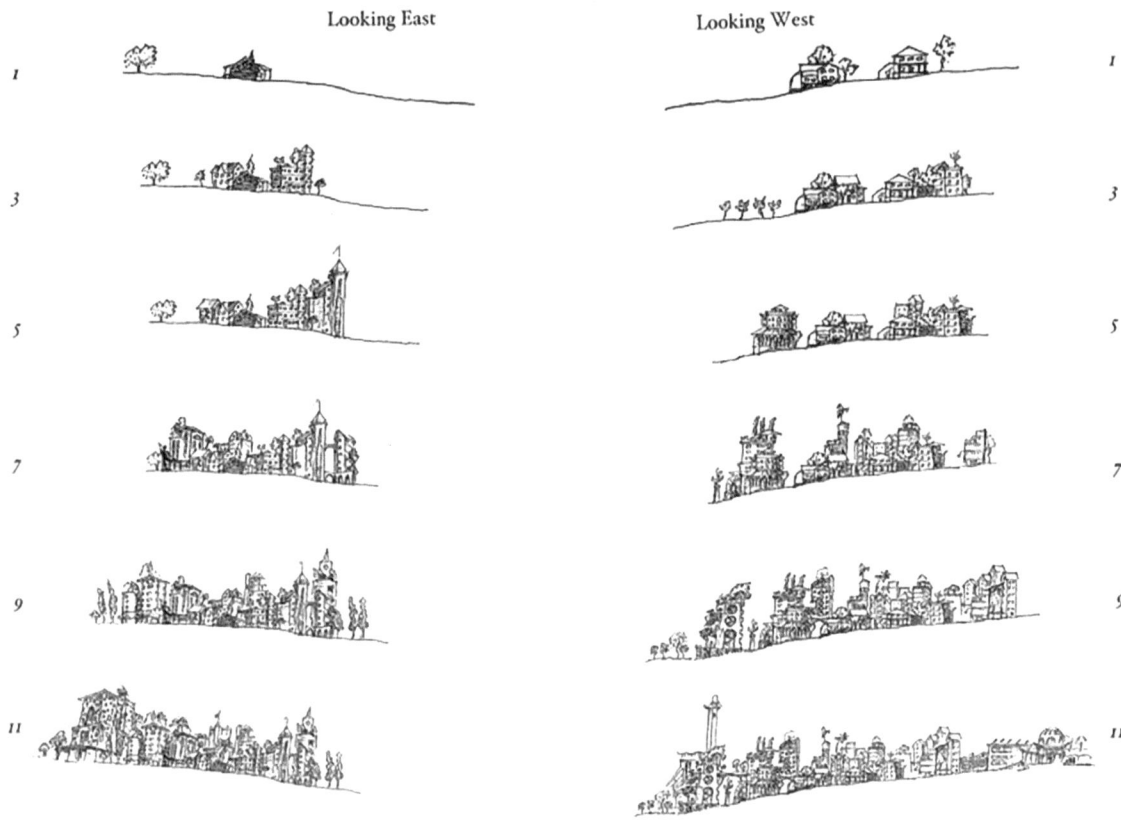

10.4 b Growing futuristic ecovillage, two elevations

In this sequence of images we can imagine standing in the middle of the plaza of the map number 1 on our previous page and if we stand facing south and look left, (or east) we see the changes over time down the left hand column of drawings above, and if we look right (or west) we see over time what is represented on the right hand column.

11.

San Francisco Bay and City – from metropolis to ecotropolis

I entered the Bay Conservation and Development Commission's "Rising Tides" competition. Mine was one in a field of 120 entries and one of three suggesting using elevated artificial fill in any way other than as a barrier to rising water, that is, as dikes and dams. Variations on dike designs garnered all prizes. My entry suggested dikes to protect only the present day higher density areas. I proposed building on artificial fill, a solution going back 4,500 years to the first cities ever built, cities of the Sumerian civilization in the Mesopotamian Valley, now in Iraq. It was the only entry to propose that building the extreme low energy pedestrian cities, towns and villages would be a major means to prevent run away sea level rise by reversing sprawl development patterns that presently produce enormous amounts of CO_2. My entry announced the coincidence of prevention and adaptation – ecocities on elevated fill – missed by all the other entries. Perhaps unsurprisingly I received no prize or honorable mention. People love responding to crisis with the tried and true patterns that lead to the crises they think they are addressing. They think the better car makes a better city. I think a better car makes a worse city. Same principle is involved in comparing dikes to ecocities on elevated hills of earth.

We could educate and plan for elevated fill with ecocity design as guidelines to transform all low lying areas of the world threatened by floods, including inland river valleys so disposed. As city, district and neighborhood centers become more diverse in function and more compact, they can be the positive growth areas contrasted to the roll back of sprawl, which is growth of nature and agriculture recovering. Shifting in this manner would be changing from today's metropolitan sprawl to "ecotropolis," introduced here on page 57, illustration 4.2 c.

The other item here in this chapter is a set of small sketches, a "story board" of sorts, of flying through a different kind of future San Francisco ecocity drawn as part of outreach efforts for the Seventh International Ecocity Conference held in San Francisco in 2008.

11.1 a Rising Tides Competition entry poster – previous page

This image is my poster entry in the 2009 Rising Tides Competition sponsored by the San Francisco Bay Conservation and Development Commission (BCDC).

11.2 b San Francisco bioregional fly through

12.

Berkeley

I lived in Berkeley, California for 29 years. Since then I've been living in Oakland between the big buildings of downtown, with Chinatown on one side and Lake Merritt on another. My efforts to think through and promote alternative futures for Berkeley resulted in my 1987 book, "Ecocity Berkeley," a scenario into the future of ecocity ideas applied to that town. Unfortunately, very little *was* applied. Here are some of the images from that book, and a few more generic or detailed ideas I worked on while there. I was focused on attempting to get projects built. A few small ones were and some zoning codes changed in a minor way but major land use and creek restoration efforts were not realized. Only a few ecocity architectural features were built. Change there was so slow and weak I shifted focus to more international work that has been steadily picking up since the early 1990s.

The ideas generated there, however, remain important and the imagery helpful. My big lesson was about how difficult it is to move comfortable even very highly educated people – maybe *especially* comfortable highly educated people – toward change regarding their neighborhoods and automobile addictive habits. Berkeley has a very democratic process replete with every imaginable commission and ordinance to promote review, re-review, re-re-review, and "new studies" built on old ones endlessly out of the past and into the future. Any serious change in real ecocity redesign and development was obstructed there. I used to joke that City Hall should have a plaque over the front door reading "Process is our most important product." We need to get beyond that mind set if we hope to build ecocities, especially "in time" to avert climate and biodiversity crises headed quickly our way.

12.1 Ecocity in Berkeley-like setting

The hills around Berkeley are now covered with a thin layer of expensive housing and trees. This image imagines withdrawing in such a landscape to the sort of mix of housing types the city presently has but with emphasis on higher density and a number of ecocity architectural features. The hills have returned to grasslands with dense forests in moist valleys along the creeks.

12.2 a The Marina becomes a bay village, far

Berkeley has a Marina built on fill and flanked on one side by a now long closed city dump covered in more or less good soil and natural regional vegetation attracting a fair number of critters including resident and migratory birds. Here (previous page and below) we see the Marina remissioned as a fishing and tourist fair-sized village.

12.2 b The Marina becomes a bay village, close

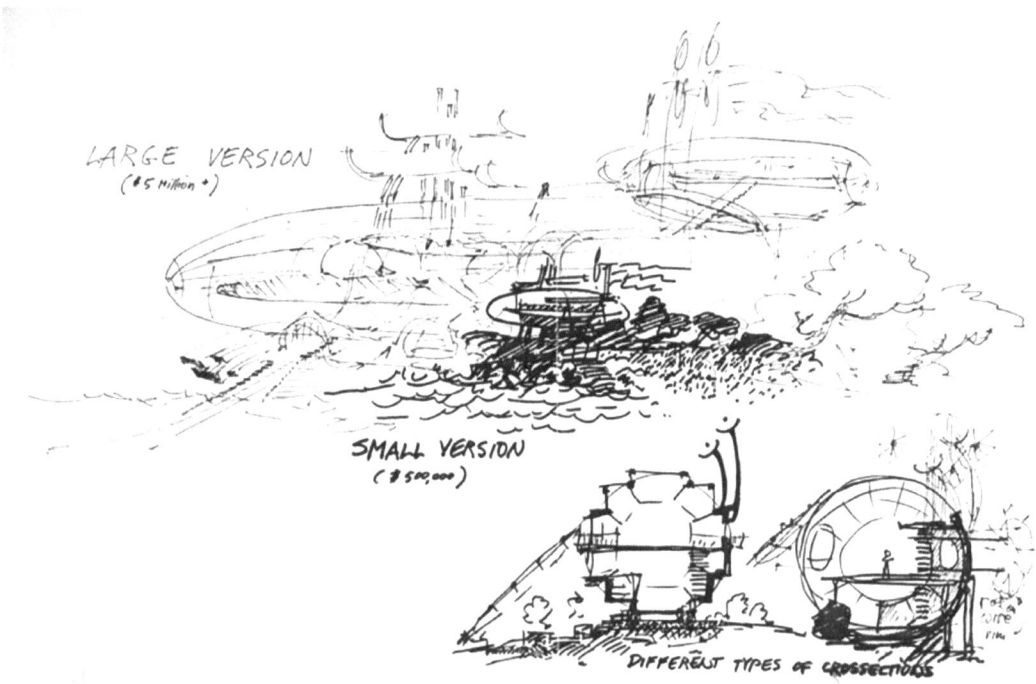

12.3 a Eco/Peace Museum and Center at Marina, sketch

North of the Marina I suggested several versions of an Eco/Peace Museum since the city was considered a leader in both movements in my early years there. The museum would model ecologically-tuned features in its design as well as in its permanent and traveling exhibits. It would also house offices, meeting rooms, a bookstore, library and shop – of both sorts, meaning a shop for fabricating exhibits and also a shop for sales of relevant items for organizations working for peace and ecological health.

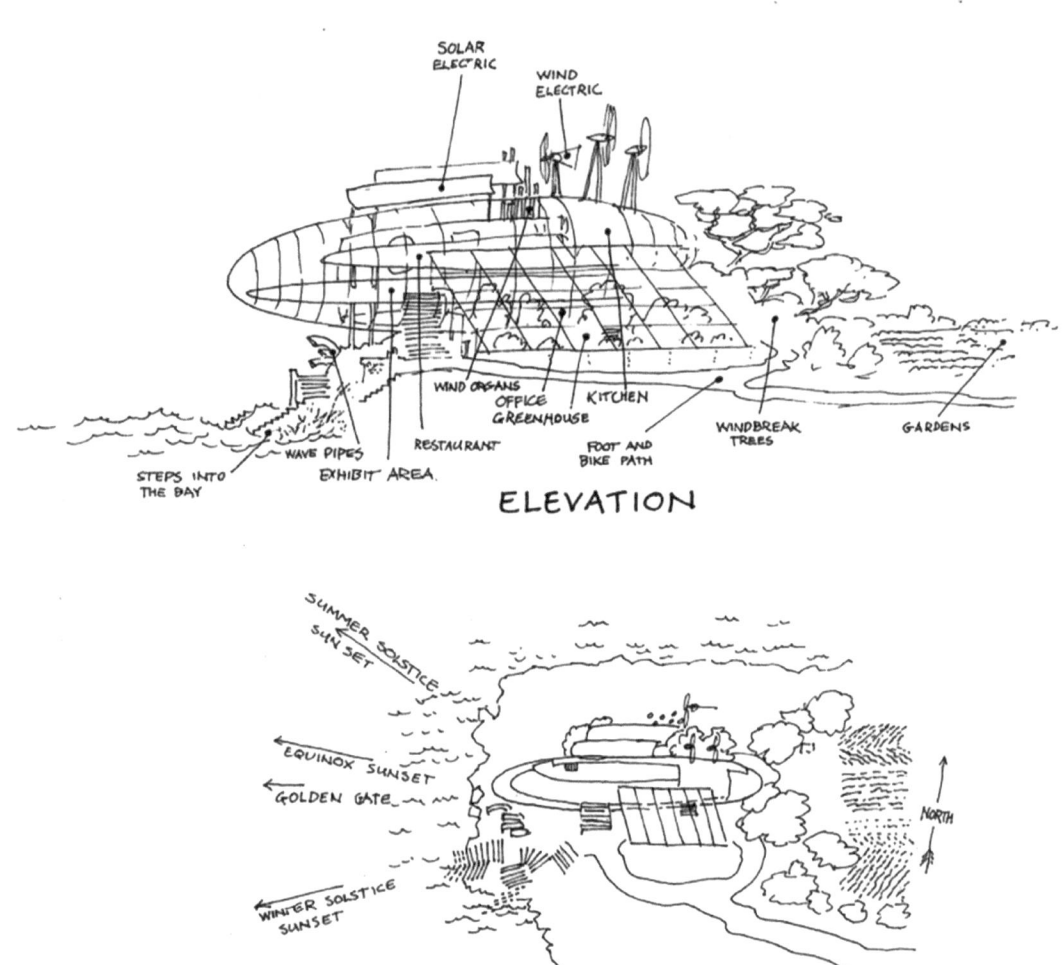

12.3 b Eco/Peace Museum and Center at Marina, line drawing

Settling in on a medium size version.

12.3 c Eco/Peace Museum and Center inside, sketch

Looking out toward the Golden Gate Bridge and Pacific Ocean beyond.

12.3 d Eco/Peace Museum and Center inside

A more developed interior drawing, in the early evening.

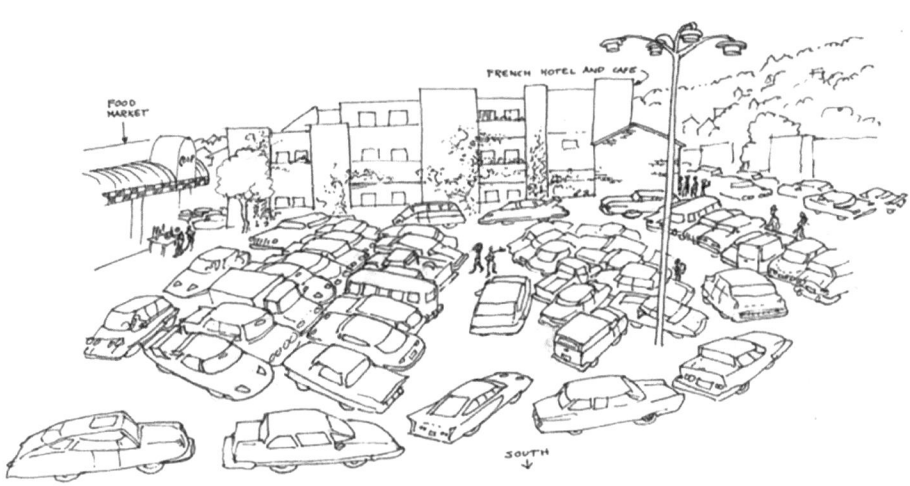

12.4 a Car parking only

The Coop food market has been replaced by an Andronico's Market. The crowded parking lot remains. My notion for change, self explanatory, below.

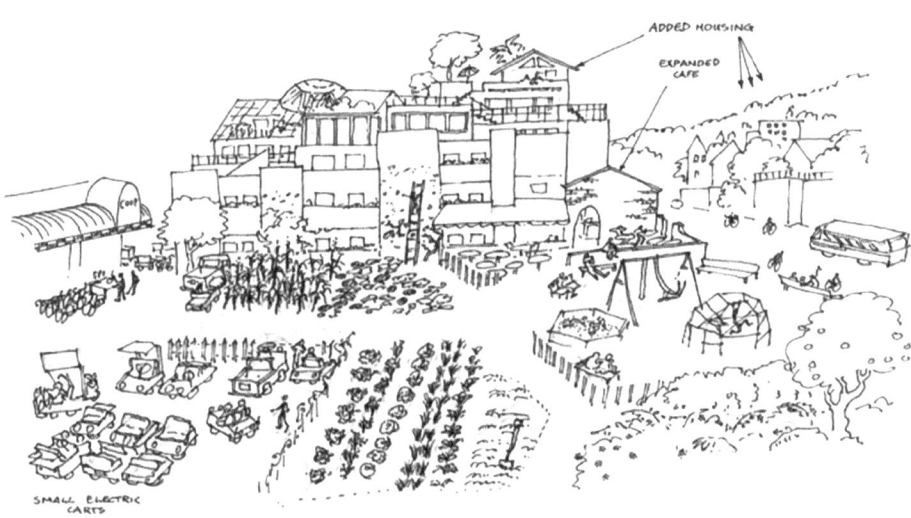

12.4 b Cart parking plus playground, garden, cafe, more people…

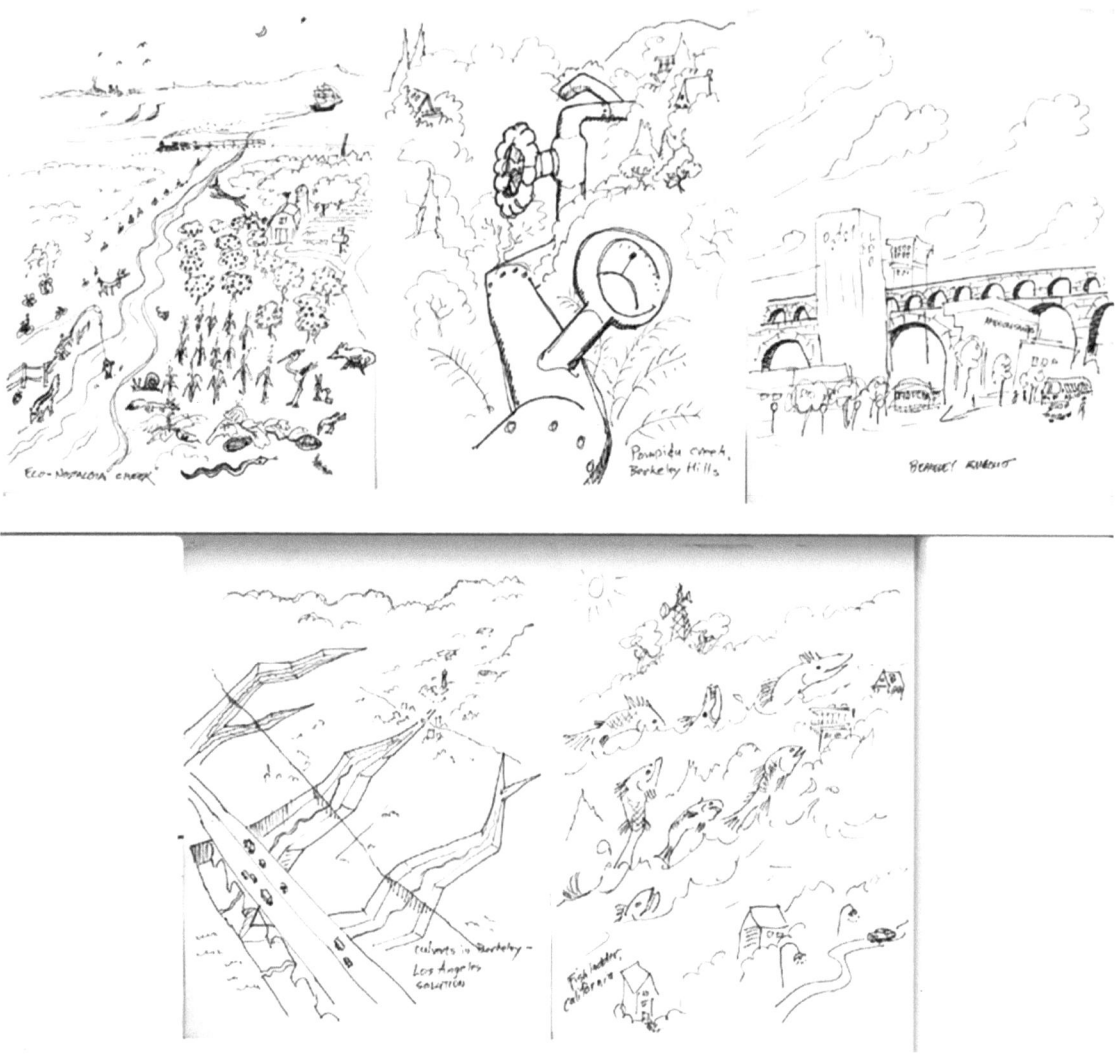

12.5 Five quick sketches of waterways at a Berkeley creek meeting

The speakers were becoming a little long-winded so I took the free time to make these sketches.

13.

Oakland

Oakland, California, a city of 380,000 people, has been my home since 2003. To further the mapping system presented in this book and its application to cities, the organization I founded, called Ecocity Builders, received a grant to work on the mapping idea with others in Oakland. The grant was from the Bay Area Air Quality Management District, the first grant ever to our knowledge for developing such a future oriented mapping system that pairs new ecologically-oriented development with projections of where to remove older automobile dependent development and where to restore important areas for natural habitat and raising food.

I also produced a long-range outline general plan for Mills College. Some of the imagery from that work is featured here.

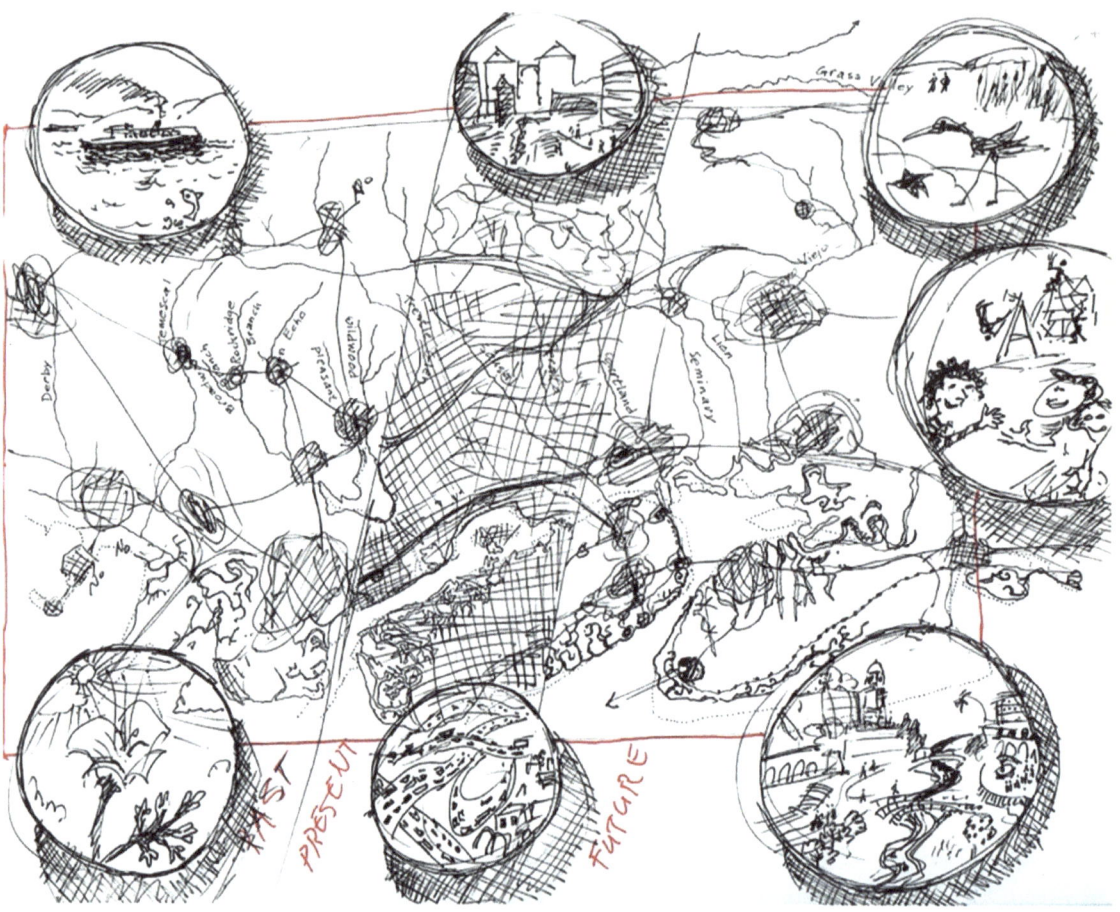

13.1 a Ecocity mapping preliminary sketch for Oakland

I was thinking of portraying the past very early city of Oakland on the left panel, a diagonal swath through the middle showing the mostly uniform low density car dependent development of today, and a future possible ecotropolis arrangement into a far healthier future.

13.1 b Past, present and future map of Oakland

The more developed version of the past, present and future map should the city be headed toward becoming an ecocity with small ecotowns and ecocity villages around it making it a new ecotropolis.

13.2 a Mills College ecotown center on Leona Creek

My proposal for Mills College was to make it more like a compact European small town, with basic shops for their kind of population, on campus living in apartments and a hotel or some bed and breakfasts for visiting friends and families.

13.2 b Ecotown Mills College, new elevated plaza

The edge of their artificial but potentially very pleasant small lake would be a very interesting place to have an elevated keyhole plaza looking out through the trees to Lake Aliso. Once again we see the thick, hard, transparent plastic skylights serving also as floors for an elevated plaza. The trees are dangerously close for fire security and so, worth it for other reasons, the sides of the buildings near the trees have exterior sprinklers – and so do the trees. This is a little expensive again but money saved on getting rid of automobile related infrastructure and waste can be invested in more graceful ways of living. Structural plastic skylights again.

13.2 c Mills elevated plaza from adjacent Lake Aliso

13.2 d Mills Lake Aliso Nature Center

This humble nature center would feature in their ecology and design curriculum. The structure includes an attached solar greenhouse, small office and classroom. The idea for the walk-down glass wall for Lake Aliso for viewing fish and other critters in the water I got from a similar built glass wall in a creek I saw and greatly enjoyed in Boise, Idaho.

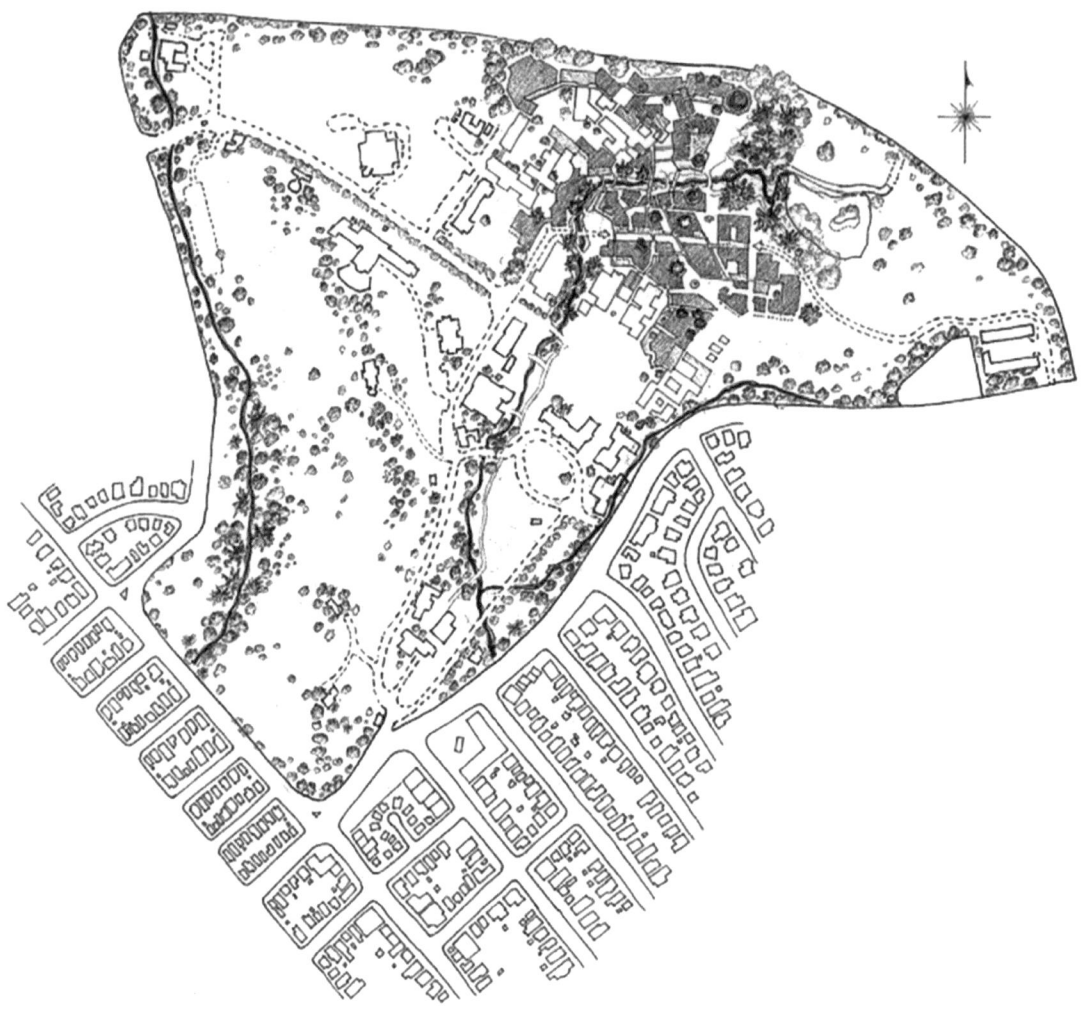

13.2 e Mills College with new development in ecocity style

Here we see the campus as a map featuring the immediately adjacent neighborhood on the south side. The campus is 135 acres in the eastern part of Oakland and has three creeks running into it, two of them joining in a confluence, then out under the neighborhood in underground culverts. The new development is portrayed in darker tones here, existing building simply as outlines. The area I'd suggest for a very mixed use new center, the real town center, is around where the darker and outlined buildings meet.

13.2 f Mills College expanding

By new City of Oakland zoning and various other inducements and gradual purchase of properties in "willing seller deals" low-density housing is removed and the creeks largely opened up toward San Francisco Bay. New apartment blocks with added interior footpaths are created for both the campus community – students and staff – but also for greater adjacent neighborhood population. This in turn justifies more variety of shops, offices and services on the southeast (lower right) flank of campus.

13.2 g Mills College creeks connecting to the Bay

Here we see further development in the neighborhood, the creeks extending to San Francisco Bay with footpaths along one side. The diagonal street in the lower left of our map, angling between the central northwest on the map and the very bottom center of the map goes under an elevated hill for a block. The hill extends the campus into a city park forming a wide area adjacent the westernmost creek course. A little more apartment development and neighborhood oriented shops are built in the adjacent town property on the east side of campus.

13.3 Grand Lake Theater area, north end of Lake Merritt

Presently an enormous freeway runs from left across this picture and all the way off the drawing to the right, creating a huge noisy barrier separating the Grand Lake center area from the lake itself. Here a streetcar line has replaced the freeway and some new higher density development fills in the shopping, restaurant and entertainment center with new development in ecocity style. Buried creeks are brought back to the surface. Over a very long time through willing seller deals, some of the lower density development is removed between centers.

14.

New Orleans, floods and other disasters

Like San Francisco Bay (and the rest of the world), New Orleans can learn a lot from the elevated fill and pedestrian design of the Sumerian Civilization 4,500 years ago – *and* the Native Americans up and down the Mississippi who added to and built upon elevated mounds to avoid floods. New Orleans also has an example of building on artificial elevated fill at the campus of the New Orleans University, which suffered no damage in the floods of Hurricane Katrina, whereas Loyola, Tulane, Xavier and other schools that were flooded suffered millions of dollars in damages. The city's French Quarter, built on a natural levee, also rises above sea level. It experienced little harm in the storm. The flooded areas were all mainly automobile dependent low-density development that cannot be raised – the land area is far too large. But take a small portion of that, say 10% or 20%, and raising a support platform of earth would be affordable. And, in an almost dead level city that is easily accessible by bicycle and that already loves its streetcar system, coordinating those modes of transport with pedestrian design and with relatively dense pedestrian development, elevated fill could solve most of the city's hurricane problems. To back off from development and let natural vegetation come back, the storm surge and waves in storms can be ameliorated.

When I went to New Orleans after Katrina almost no one wanted to even begin discussing any land use changes. The situation remains, though more and more people are realizing their choices for recovery are still not working well.

Elevated fill and pedestrian/ecocity design works for towns that suffer tsunamis too. And compact development in fire landscapes provides, with an open buffer zone, swimming pools and water pumps, good defense from fires. This idea I brought before Oakland and Berkeley officials and the public after the firestorm disaster of 1991 that destroyed 3,375 homes in the hills east of those two cities. The idea was not implemented – but would work! A version of the same idea is featured here representing a community built on the hills overlooking Santa Barbara, California.

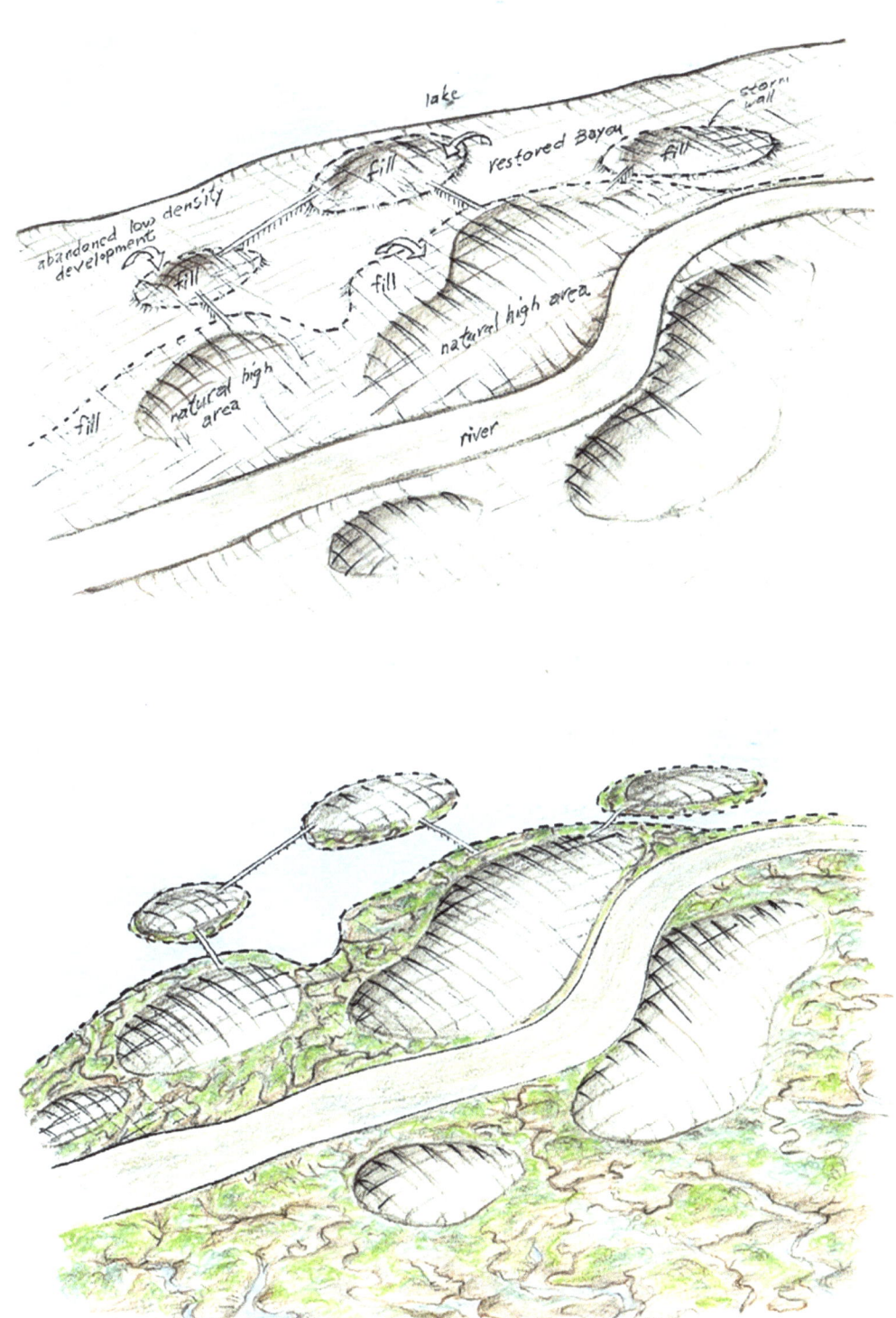

14.1 a Basic idea for elevating land and compact development

The concept here is to build more compactly in finite development areas surrounded by new marshy lands that blunt the impact of storms.

14.1 b Bring back natural waters and plants, make island arts centers

The new natural marshy areas could have walkways to "art islands" where poetry, music and other inspiring events could be held. The storm comes. Then build it over again. The damage in this strategy of city building would be trivial compared to what such low lying cities suffer now in extreme flood or will suffer in climate change conditions.

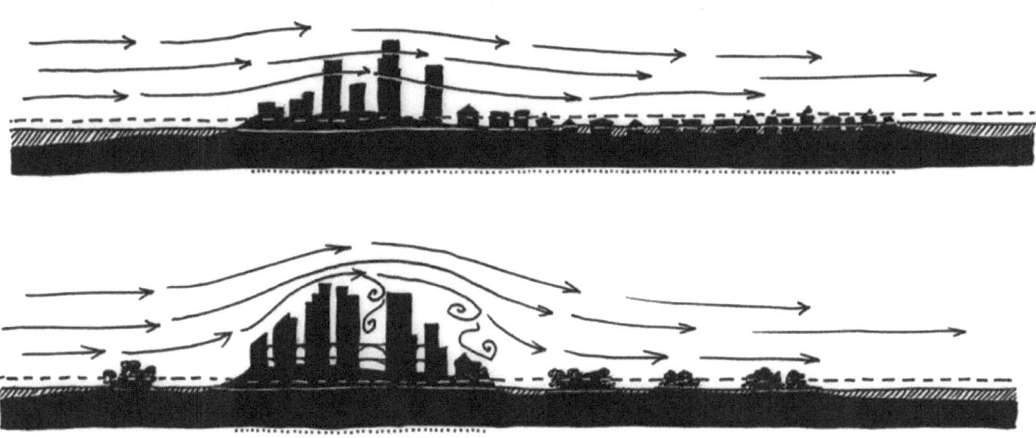

14.1 c Hill, shell and labyrinth: solution for hurricane cities

Artificial hills can raise communities above floods, and streets can be patterned to break winds with "T" intersections and curving layout. In addition, with compact development, only building surfaces facing the outside edge need to be hard shell covered. Below, a whole new neighborhood turning into a city center could be built on islands linked mainly by transit to other centers.

14.1 d New island neighborhood on dredge and fill

14.1 e A new quarter rises on elevated earth

People love their streetcar system in New Orleans – fits perfectly with the higher density mixed use centers that could be built on artificial earthen platforms. Here we see one of the small arts features on the wetlands nearby, illustration 14.1 b, page 146, and can note in the upper center and center right staircases that go down about 20 feet to the natural level of the area. Come the big hurricanes, clear off rooftop furniture into sheltered upper level spaces, to be returned to rooftops after the storm has passed.

14.1 f Rainbow Girl sculpture for edge of Lake Pontchartrain

On the north side of New Orleans is the enormous Lake Pontchartrain, which is actually an inlet of the Gulf of Mexico. There could be a sculpture there, celebrating the spirit of surviving the weather, a fountain producing the right sized droplets to produce a rainbow when the sun is shining. When the storm is bearing down, a maintenance person could simply unscrew the umbrella and replace it after the storm has passed through. The drawing shows high and low tides, the two lower lines, and storm surge, the upper water line with larger waves.

14.2 Build on artificial earthen mound to avoid tsunamis, too

Rising above tsunamis can protect villages, towns and cities from floods. Heap up "clean fill" and cover with a coat of concrete or thick masonry; build pedestrian ecocity infrastructure on top. The small dock, boats and light shelters on the beach will be swept away but the people can head up the stairs to escape all but the most stunningly high tsunamis possible. Some people build in funnel shaped valleys that amplify the height of tsunamis, which is the worst possible location. Don't do that!

14.3 a Fire safe village for Mediterranean climates

Compact development also works well for defense of communities in firestorm areas of Mediterranean climates like the south of France, Greece, coastal California and much of Australia. This illustration imagines the California coastline at Santa Barbara with the Channel Islands on the horizon. Fire winds almost always come from approximately the same direction. On that side of the community a swimming pool or several can be built and fires fought with gasoline powered water pumps, hoses and nozzles. Some water has to be directed toward the infrastructure itself to put out incendiaries like fiery twigs that updraft from superheated air throw downwind to start small fires ahead of the main wall of flame. The larger number of people relative to the area to be defended and the smallness of the development's footprint when in the form of an ecological community work for much easier defense than scattered single family homes that burn in the thousands around the world every year, scattered out into flammable, seasonally dry landscapes.

14.4 b Firefighting close up

Many people, small land area to defend, swimming pools for water, pumps, hoses and nozzles make for effective firefighting; isolated houses not so much.

15.

Key projects underway

One is definitely underway: Tianjin Eco-city for 350,000 people on the coast of the Bohai Sea directly east of Beijing. A second is a mature design, if not committed project, and underway in that sense. It was sponsored initially by the Ministry of Works and Human Settlement in that mystic but ever so real and relevant Kingdom of Gross National Happiness high in the Himalayas, Bhutan. I was invited to help them design a small ecocity, traveled there and produced what you will see following shortly. A third project is Ecocity Detroit, Michigan which I'm dragging kicking and screaming toward reluctant leadership in the history of cities and cars. I don't know if I'll succeed or if they will. The grand scheme there: as the city that kick-started the whole world of automobile dominated and car dependent cities, what other town could be better to lead toward the healthy, happy, ecocity civilization of the future? I've been there two times meeting key opinion, environmentalist, gardening and development leaders. But will they, with my prodding, lead in the mission to build infinitely better cities? So regarding Detroit, you are in on the beginning there, and let's hope it is not stillborn but rather plays out a religious conversion turning its genius from dubious and contradictory to modeling the "Generous City, City of the Future."

About that term, slogan even, that is precisely the most important vision for future cities I can imagine. The most basic thing we need to do in relation to our built environment, the home on Earth that we build, is to understand it is now time to give back – as a matter of survival as well as "thrival." Our beautiful planet manifesting the lifeblood of Nature Herself, in physics, math, chemistry, evolution and ecology, has given us life in amazing fullness. If we don't understand our obligation to now be generous and give back, maybe we deserve to be doomed. But those who go down with us, most no doubt before us, as thousands of species have disappeared from existence because of us people already, certainly don't deserve extinction. We need to understand we can build infinitely better.

For such understanding we need education more than anything else, education about ecology on the planet and building as giving back in return for the gift of life itself. And the best of education comes from actually doing something, in our subject in this book in particular, the class of doing called building something, leading and teaching through action and not just words.

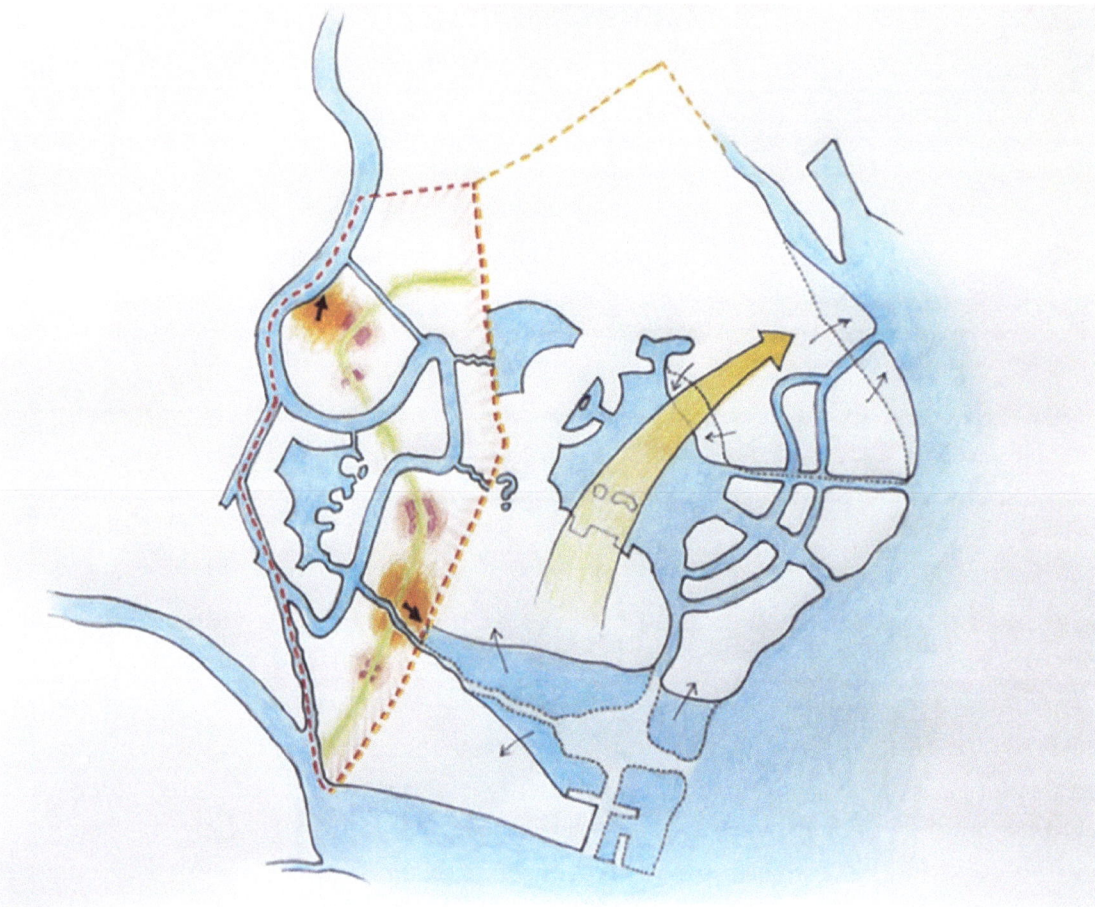

15.1 a Adjusting the map of Tianjin Eco-City

I was hired to write an assessment of Tianjin Eco-City three years into actual construction. My report congratulated the project for many ecocity features including higher density in the current Chinese way of city building plus a high degree of mixed uses, an effort to implement maximum transit, a bicycle and foot path called the "Green Valley" running throughout the project (the yellow green line above), solar and wind energy technology, restoration of habitat for natural species eliminated nearby because of recent and earlier extirpation, and so on. Since much was built that already could not be changed I looked to the plans and saw, to my discouragement, that there was not going to be a coastline on the water: another development is planned on raised earth of even larger size.

In the map above the ecocity project is within the dashed red line. The future project blocking the sea is to the east (right) surrounded by a yellow dashed line and blue water. Where you see a dark blue wedge shape of water is where I suggested removing fill (or not placing it there in the first place) and shifting it as indicated by the large yellow arrow and thin black arrows so as to open up the view to the sea from a future keyhole plaza: the lower orange dot with small black arrow pointing out toward the view. I suggested, along with more ideas not included here, another such plaza, above and slightly to the left looking up river.

15.1 b An elevated double layered keyhole plaza

This drawing imagines a cross section view through the "wedge" in the future ocean-blocking development (would be "blocking" if built in the way presently planned anyway) and a keyhole plaza over two large interior public/commercial spaces. The large circle holes are either open skylights or thick, strong plastic items people can walk on. In this scheme there would be three stories height between the broad floor plates pictured here as sliced through for seeing interior details. Two very large native species sculptures and relatively tall buildings flank the view seaward, emphasizing and celebrating the view: a good location for a certain amount of tourism.

15.1 c Amending the large buildings only, wide streets pattern

These days new Chinese cities are going up extremely rapidly with large, massive buildings, a means to house and provide employment space for many people in order to solve problems of rural poverty and speed economic development, creating the infrastructure for an urban migration unprecedented in history. In addition, the streets are very wide and the blocks several times larger than typical American blocks and many times larger than the blocks of European cities created in a time when everyone walked, with a few sometimes riding horses or carriages.

A little more fine grain development would complement that approach and add more intimate friendly spaces while greatly reducing mechanized traffic and the excessive use of energy because of the cars and trucks encouraged by such design. Above, the gray shapes schematically represent the large buildings of the Tianjin Eco-city project, and the blue shapes represent somewhat smaller infill buildings. The extra wide streets running along the limits of the very large superblocks are represented by the dotted lines. My suggestion relative to the streets is to make them narrower, defined by the light gray lines and green open space thus created. The yellow orange areas are new public spaces opened up for a variety of uses created by the sheltering shapes of the new configuration of buildings and street-encroaching curb lines. The existing and planned interior walkways, in my version, cross streets mid block, blocking and slowing motorized traffic, creating a much more pedestrian friendly environment.

15.2 a Location for a possible ecotown in Bhutan

Above we have a Google Earth image of a portion of the Panbang valley (pronounced with a soft "a" more like Pon-bong), plus yellow orange dotted lines defining the rough area to be planned if my ecocity thoughts for the area pan out. The pink dotted line represents a bluff about 125 feet high with almost flat land above the bluff and again almost flat land below the bluff. The new national highway is a white line, actually photographically looking that way, only the second east west highway to connect the country, probably the only country in the world without a street light signal. The road is a fairly narrow two-lane affair. About twelve farm houses and some small farms share the space with wild lands at the present. We can see the confluence of two rivers here, only four miles from the Bhutan southern border with India and barely 300 feet above sea level.

My challenge was to layout and provide some preliminary design detailing for a small but complete ecotown harmonious the with country's Gross National Happiness values and policies. The economy would be local farming in this hot wet climate, some ecotourism and sports facilities. I also proposed a small campus of a thoroughgoing ecocity educational institute, perhaps a branch campus of an existing college or university.

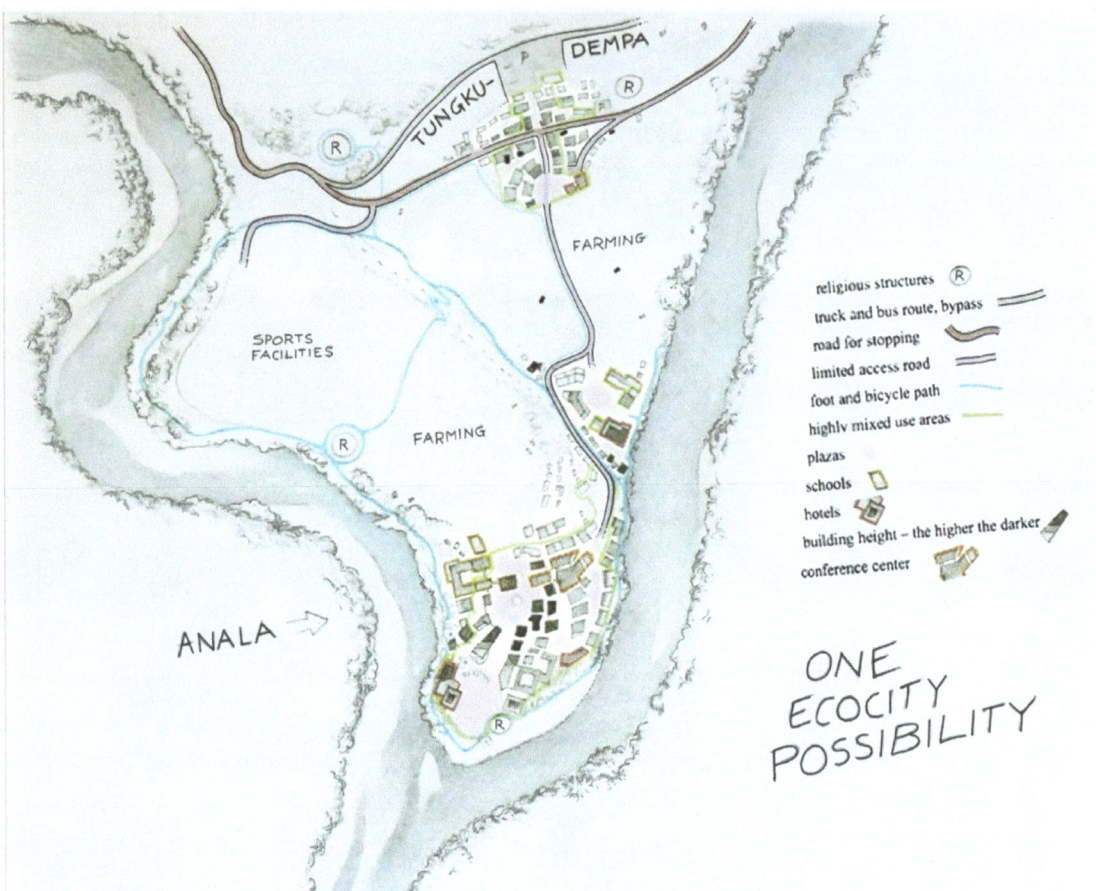

15.2 b   A thoroughly pedestrian design

My friends in the Ministry of Works and Human Settlement envisioned twin towns with the northern portion relating directly to the new national road, with parking, and with a commercial emphasis appropriate to the highway and local farming and crafts production. The rest of the development would be car-free except for delivery, mostly by truck. The layout is based on relatively dense development of the sort seen in the capital city of Thimphu, narrow streets and public plazas, three of them keyhole plazas. Two thirds of the land would be left in agriculture and a very minimum of farmers would be displaced and offered places in the town and some of the presently not cultivated open space, to be shared with sports facilities and native plant and animal areas, though the entire enormous region of the Manas Tiger Reserve surrounds, managed by the Bhutan and Indian governments on their respective sides of the border.

Plazas are in pink, walking and bicycling trail in bright blue, the dashed gray line represents the bluff demarking the upper and lower nearly flat plateaus. The Rs represent religious and/or cultural structures of local veneration.

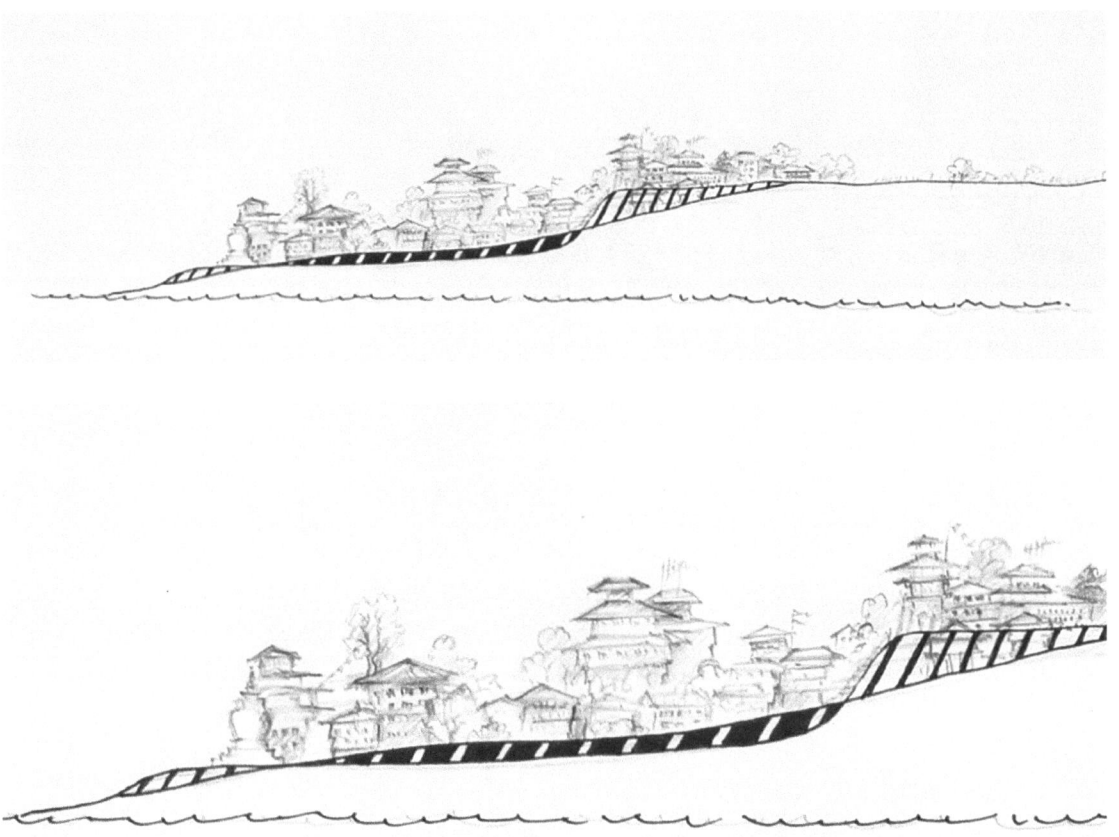

15.2 c Cross section of Anala, the lower of the two town centers

This drawing shows cut (black diagonal stripes on white) and fill (white diagonal stripes on black) to create a more generally sloped and unified Anala that provides best views toward the confluence of rivers merging and heading south through the last gap in the Bhutan mountains and into India on the water's way to the vast Bay of Bengal. The idea is to respect nature there and the local architecture detailing, emphasize the aspects of it that relate sensitively to the conditions of intense sun and rain and model the ecocity layout and design features that create the best possible positive impact on both nature and culture in that location.

15.2 d Cross section of Anala, the lower of the two town centers

Imagining splitting the southern end of Anala down the middle of the plaza with the view to the confluence of the rivers, the Dangmechu on the east and the Mangdechu on the west becoming the Manas River headed south. Here we see schematics of bridges connecting buildings on the second and third floor level and the basic forms typical of several classes of Bhutanese structures. The bridges and associated terraces are highlighted in the lower of the two images. A raised planter is also highlighted, similar to ones typical in many Himalayan and northern Indian towns but in this case raised even higher than typical, to celebrate a large tree of meaning to the local people.

15.2 e Zooming in on rooftop details

    The concept here is to utilize the basic lines and esthetics typical in Bhutanese architecture with addition of harmonious ecocity features. For example, in Bhutan there are as a rule broad overhanging roofs of a shallow slope that look like they are floating a foot or two over the flat roof of the top occupied floor. The spaces under these roofs are open to the air and create cool shade and protection from rain for dried food and storage of many other things. These eaves are wide enough to provide a good measure of shelter in the streets from rain and sun of the sort that drenches the Anala and Tungkudempa sites in their Panbang valley. In a variation on the theme and respecting the interest there in cultivating ecotourism, I'm suggesting raising the roof another five or six feet and creating well sheltered space with surrounding perspectives open to the viewing pleasure of locals and tourists, students, teachers, athletes, farmers and ecocity designers… many sorts of people. In the above design, transparent skylights allow the sun to shine on a small restaurant's roof, providing indirect lighting under the "floating roof." A two level bridge, left, connects the two buildings.

15.3 a Basic form of Detroit – and thousands of other car dominated cities

In other words, flat low-density development served with enormous commitment to asphalt and concrete, abstracted here in the form of streets and sidewalks.

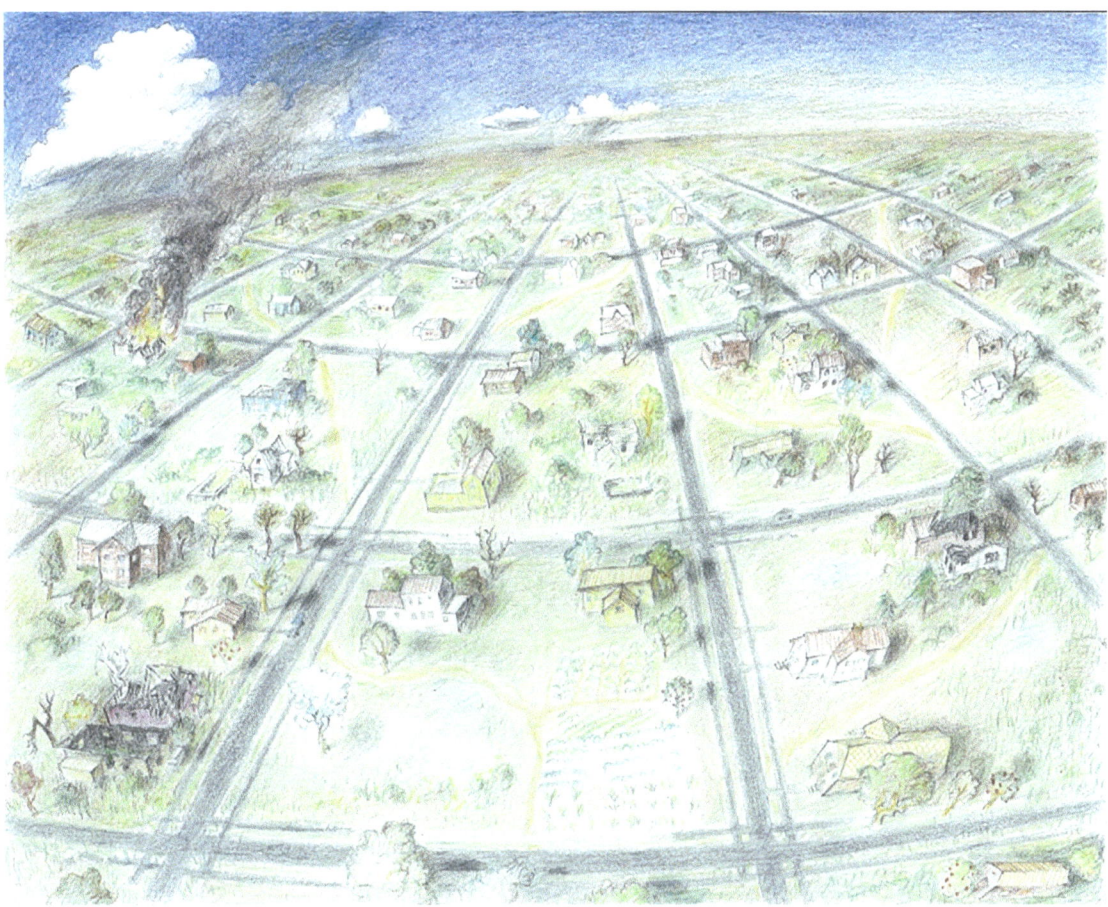

15.3 b Slowly disintegrating since the 1960s

Detroit provided the first massive outpouring of cars to the world and thus reshaped cities in radical dependence on cars, gasoline and enormous amounts of land. Once laid out for cars, life without cars became extraordinarily difficult in cities around the world – and the rest is history. For those with an environmental conscience and those with a desire for rich, face to face urban life, I'm suggesting starting off in Detroit with a small integral neighborhood, aka, ecocity fractal.

Presently the city, outside of its present downtown, has proportions of old development, derelict property and open space very similar to the drawing above. Collapse from disinvestment started when the automobile companies fled the United States with most of the manufacture following lowest price "globalized" economics looking for and finding low cost workers thousands of miles away. The local result is enormous amounts of open space and cheap land and, should visionaries and investors come together, the potential of taking the world lead – a new story – in setting the stage for a genuinely healthy and happy "ecocity civilization," a term a number of Chinese are beginning to use when talking about a possible ecocity future.

15.3 c Ecocity "fractal" or whole small town within town

An ecocity fractal is a development project from the minimum scale of two or three blocks on up to maybe ten or twenty blocks that has all the essential components of a functionally complete city or town present and well arranged. This one has the equivalent of about six blocks of medium density development.

15.3 d Plaza and street experience

Above we have the same design as on the previous page but emphasizing, in pink, the open (left plaza) and closed (right plaza) experiences. The streets are highlighted in blue here to give a sense of where the more closed, close-in pedestrian feel is the sense of the built environment. In just a few steps the pedestrian is in a natural or agricultural world.

Last comment about the three projects just described – I consider getting a project built of the sort these three represent as one of the most crucial human endeavors before us for survival and thriving on this beleaguered planet, beleaguered only because of what people have been doing "wrong" or at least with very little consciousness of consequences and conscience to face a particular set of life and death facts for all life forms here. In my travels speaking in 35 countries now I have found no place where an ecocity project is genuinely complete in possessing all of its essential components, much less optimally arranged and tuned appropriately to its local conditions. And, the built environment of cities, towns and villages constitutes the largest creation of our species. That fact alone indicates that it is absolutely essential to deal clearly and directly with ecocity projects as a survival issue.

15.3e Creating close-in nature and farm

This version of the Detroit ecocity fractal proposal is about 1/3 the amount of human shelter as shown in illustration 15.3 c and d. Here we have more natural habitat in close: the patch of dense forest on the right side of the drawing. It also shows more agriculture on the left side of the small development. One of the virtues of ecocity communities of a wide range of scales that escapes most casual observers is how important and also how easy it is in such a development to simply step a few feet outside and, there you are in the natural or food and fiber-supplying environment with much calm and essential knowledge to imbibe. And, just catch the streetcar to downtown or other neighborhood centers becoming ecotowns or ecovillages.

16.

Nature and garden

Nature, biology, food, water, e nergy… What's it all about after all, the city that actually enhances nature, in trade for all human nurture? Why can't cities be a net contribution to biodiversity and ecological health as those are to us? What about the generous city, the one that gives back? It's a matter of designing them that way. Human beings produce kitchen, agricultural, body and various other organic wastes with which to build soil. We can plant native gardens to attract native species, and even in apartments have window boxes if our landlords won't stop us, and we can plant on the rooftops… sometimes. Our diets can be mainly or wholly vegetarian and/or organic, sourced locally mainly or emphasized seasonally with what grows best when. With non-toxics, assiduous recycling and design to conserve land and energy while using renewable energy technology we can benefit nature as well as our own cultural evolution. We can create soil and regenerate natural habitat and species. Local food and farmers markets *are* good ideas. We can make room for them instead of asphalt and car dependent development by simply giving them room – by building the city that covers little land while serving people much better at the same time.

Basically, nature's economy is primary. Ours is derivative. It's the law, the ultimate law!

16.1 Some native species, San Francisco Bay Area

A drawing for the Mills College "outline general plan proposal." Pretty much the way it looked before the college was built.

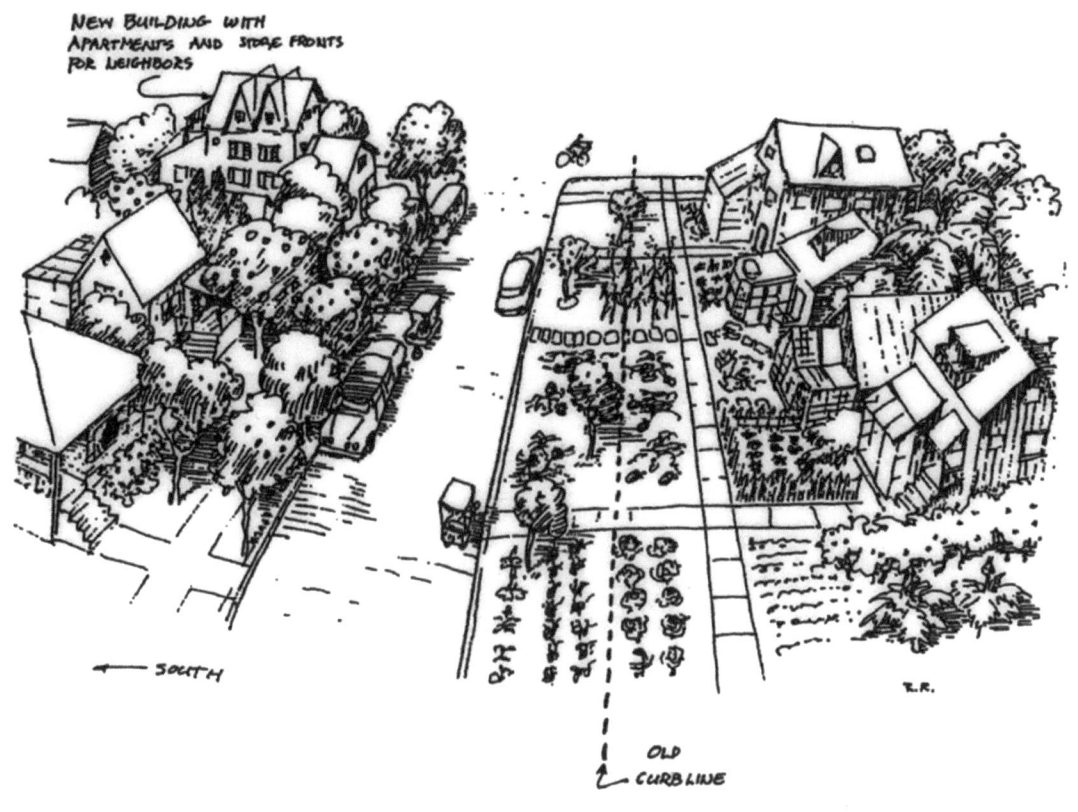

16.2 Make streets narrow, add orchard and food garden

Why not orchards in the streets? On the shady side, the side on the left here, it's a perfect place for fruit production, managed by some agreement either by owners or the city. There are "Parks and Rec" departments or Public Works maintaining trees. Why not a program with urban orchardists to care for and teach about proper care of fruit trees and harvest for probably not a large but a significant amount of production in many places, even some areas of public parks? Add to urban orchards community gardens for apartment dwellers and roof-top plots as well.

This drawing imagines the sunny side of the street gaining about 18 more feet for garden – choice of planting to the owners, renters or by agreement to share with neighbors. Many possibilities. There is room for native plants hosting local birds, animals and insects too.

16.3 Urban street nut harvester

Off center motor shakes the tree. Rakes and shovels harvest.

16.4 Orchard over freeway

When I drew this picture around 1983 I thought of it as a kind of fanciful joke. But considering the damage to the world caused by cars it seemed a lesson dwelt therein. Then ten years later I saw exactly the same design built and functioning on the northeast bank of the Danube River in Vienna, Austria complete with the box-like air vents rising high enough so that the people wouldn't be very tempted to climb up on them and fall in. There was an open grassy park above the freeway, however. Could be an orchard.

16.5 Book cover illustration for Ecocity Berkeley

This drawing was on the cover of my 1987 book Ecocity Berkeley – "Building Cities for a Healthy Future."

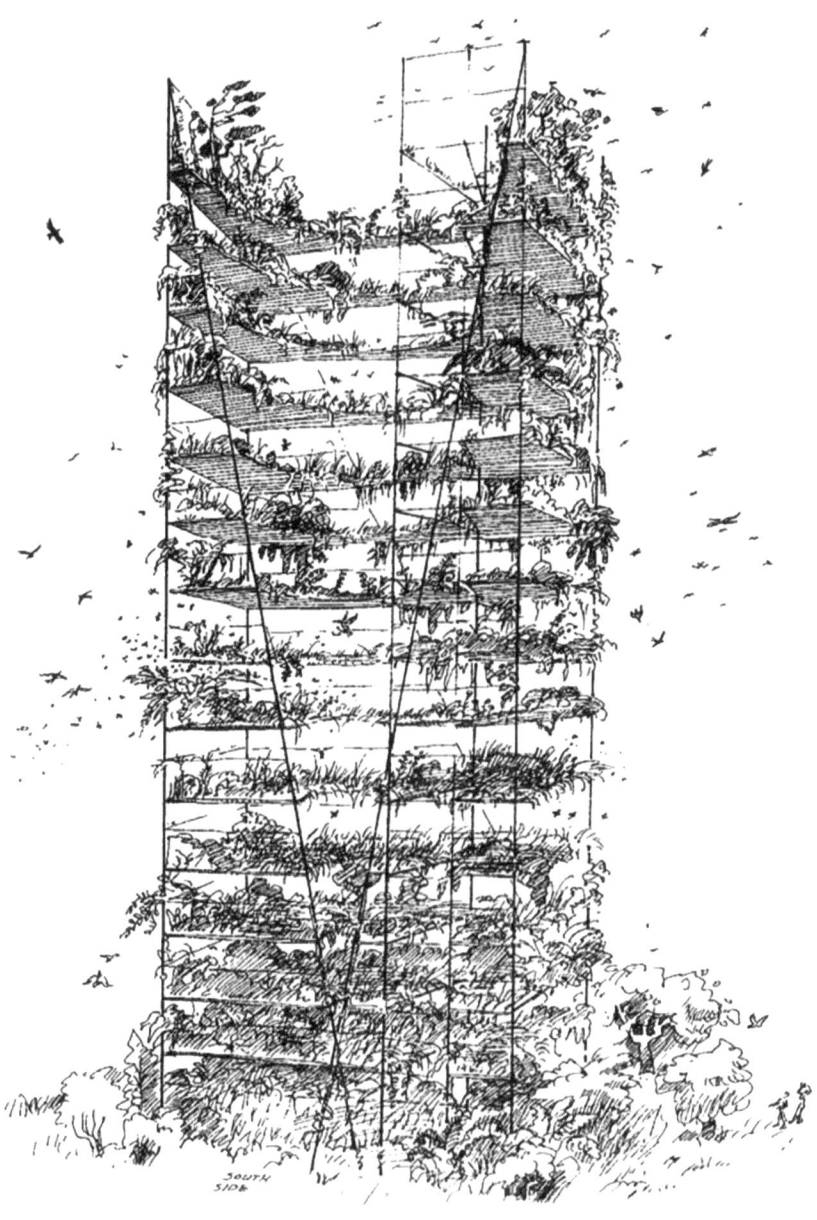

16.6 Birdhouse for large urban park

    I'd heard of buildings from the construction boom and collapse around 1926 and '27, harbinger of the Crash of 1929 and that they were deserted in mid construction and stayed there for decades. That was in Florida and the bust left a number of incomplete tall skeleton buildings that my informants said ended up being apartment houses for local plants and animals, different ones on different floors. Would be interesting to build one in a public park to be watched with binoculars. People stay back. Natural history unfolding, evolving. A kind of eco-artwork.

16.7 Colin Davis at restored creek, Berkeley, Albany border in California

Local child enjoys a parking lot. It was, in any case a parking lot two years earlier. At the time pictured above, around 1996, the creek had been recently opened to the sky, clouds, sunshine, moon and stars. With the waters, fish, crawdads, dragonflies, and dozens of bird species had replaced the parking lot at the location. As I write in 2016 there are now 40 foot willows and alders and a succession of all sorts of other species, volunteers and random strollers come by to pick fruit from the adjacent orchard and… enjoy.

16.8 Space city down to earth.

As a child I loved the idea of space travel, rockets to the moon, space cities somewhat like the one depicted here. Later I drew a sketchy cartoon I thought might be a grounded notion, if basically a science fiction version for the sort of fun a child might have like Colin in the last drawing, well-grounded like Colin in the garden with sunflowers by the restored creek, while space age imaginative at the same time. I lost the original sketch but the idea lingered on and a few years ago I enjoyed taking this Photoshop flight of fantasy based on a picture I took of cows grazing in Montana and a couple other images in bringing the future down to Earth if in only symbolic form.

17.

Sculptural city

I was a happy sculptor and planning on enjoying staying that way about the time I met Paolo Soleri, as I mentioned in the introduction to this book. Then, as early as 1965 I started thinking about the enormous need to wake people up to ecocity design. I had two major reasons: to help further evolution of human creativity in the most positive way and as a means to cease the destruction of the planet. No joke! I took it seriously, and still do: 1. cities as a means to higher creative and compassionate individuals and society, and, 2. cities to solve our most pressing problems, even save us from catastrophe. And meantime throughout I have thought of the city rather like three-dimensional works of sculptural art to be lived in and appreciated as such.

17.1 Nature on and all around

17.2 Rainbow prism aqueduct water sculpture

Always liking spectral displays (often called "rainbows" though only real rainbows are that particular *type* of spectral display), I thought water prisms like those shown above, throwing shimmering rainbow colors into a pond, would be a pleasure for all, creating you might say, double shimmering reflections off the water on whoever and whatever might be around. Add fish and frogs, native reeds. High tech plastics again, rather than producing the smog and CO_2 and climate change from burning. Another virtue of ecocity ways of building.

17.3 Creek environment with bioregional sculpture

Here we have a slice of life from the Heart of the City project offered in Berkeley, California. In this version, in the foreground the creek is in the open and focus of public attention and pleasure. On the right, and upstream, it is passing through a narrow alley in a much more intimate relationship with people. The variety adds richness to the whole city.

17.4 Bioregional sculpture near creek

Conclusion

Now from the two dimensions of the sheets of paper of this book we rise up from the flat representation to the building of the three-dimensional ecocity itself. There are enough tools and imagery here to power that transition. Nothing exotic or not yet discovered or developed required. All we need is the decision to live peacefully with the rest of nature. Together we can build a better world. Peace on Earth, peace *with* Earth.

Acknowledgments

Since this book was drawn and pondered over a period of 40 years, to whom it is indebted is practically endless. Let's call them the creative and conscientious I've chanced upon in my good luck to have been born in important times among wonderfully creative people. Special thanks for important recent help for my work to Ken King, publisher of "Vertical Cities – a Solution for Sustainable Living" in which several of my drawings are featured. Beyond that, I'd like to thank all those who have actually hired me to think, draw, write and talk. But in regard to this book in particular, my thanks to the Foundation for Sustainability and Innovation for helping to sustain me and encouraging my innovations more than any others, and over more than 20 years now. Special thanks to Stacy Becker for proofing and Charles Feldman for book design.

About the Author

Richard Register believes cities can build soil and restore biodiversity and biomass to a human-beleaguered world. We can contribute to healthy evolution on our home planet. We can create a creative future. Above all else he strives for "Peace on Earth, Peace *with* Earth." He lives in Oakland, California.

www.ingramcontent.com/pod-product-compliance
Lightning Source LLC
Chambersburg PA
CBHW041509220426
43661CB00047B/1517